CANAL TUNNELS OF ENGLAND & WALES

David Appleby
Allan Gilbert
Paul Samuel

*A*ylestone

First published in 2001 by Aylestone.

Typeset by Click-Click Interactive Ltd.
Printed in the United Kingdom by Birkenhead Press Ltd.

A catalogue record for this book is available from the British Library.

ISBN 0 9540382 0 7

A **ylestone**

(an imprint of Click-Click Interactive Ltd.)
Unit 13 Fazeley Industrial Estate
160 Fazeley Road
Birmingham B5 5RS.

info@clickx2.freeserve.co.uk.

CANAL TUNNELS OF ENGLAND & WALES

ACKNOWLEDGEMENTS

This project would not have been possible without the help and encouragement of the following people and organisations, as well as many others (particularly publicans) the authors met and talked to whilst pottering around various canals up and down the country.

Thank you all.

Brian Holden (Rochdale Canal Society); Dick Booth (Callis Mill); Andy Griffin; Doug Small & Peter Smith (Wilts & Berks Canal Amenities Group); Derek Gilbert (Precision Component Blasting, Birmingham); Lynda Gilbert; British Waterways Archives, Gloucester Docks; The Portland Basin Museum, Ashton-under-Lyne; The Black Country Living Museum, Dudley; The Canal Shop, Second City Canal Cruises, Birmingham; Huddersfield Canal Society; Lancashire Mining Museum, Salford; Cotswold Canal Trust; the staff at High Peak Junction, Cromford Canal; John Fellows; Roy Bailey and family; British Waterways...

...and the inhabitants, boaters, fishermen and gongoozlers around various canal tunnels of England and Wales.

Needless to say, any mistakes or omissions that have survived several stages of proof-reading remain the fault of the authors!

CANAL TUNNELS OF ENGLAND & WALES

CONTENTS

INTRODUCTION

A tunnel is defined by the Oxford English Dictionary as

A subterranean passage, a roadway excavated underground esp. under a hill or mountain, or beneath the bed of a river: now most commonly a railway; also, on a canal, in a mine, etc.

There is no dispute about the many brick-lined worm holes over a mile long that are scattered about the canalways all over England and Wales. The grey area arises when examining shorter structures, especially when they look like or are shorter than similar wide bridges.

John Gagg, author of the book 'Canal Tunnels', avoids defining what constitutes a tunnel. He does say in the section on Galton and Summit 'tunnels' that: "If you think of a tunnel as a hole bored through a hill, then these two aren't really tunnels. But what else are they ?". The debate centres around the fact that Summit and Galton were later additions to sections which had been in water for many years, and because they were created by covering the site with a concrete tube which was then covered over with earth.

▲ *Inside Summit tunnel*

In 1994 a report on tunnel safety compiled for the Health and Safety Executive defined a tunnel as "A structure covering over the canal for more than 50 metres". By this definition Snow Hill in Birmingham would qualify - but you won't find any pages on Snow Hill here - we think it's a viaduct ! The Proof House viaducts in the centre of Birmingham look like a tunnel close up and from inside, but from a distance – it's a viaduct ! Of course, if it were a tunnel, it would be longer than fifty of the 'true tunnels' in this book - many of which would not qualify under the HSE 1994 definition.

▲ *Proof House viaduct portal*

Confused? See for yourself the variety. Over one hundred tunnels featured in this book... from Standedge at 5,210 metres through solid Pennine rock to Dunsley at just 23 metres length; - from Deansgate - all steel and concrete, to Sapperton - mostly unlined, hacked from limestone; from Blisworth with only occasional shafts up to the surface, to Dudley's sunlit caverns and Fenny Compton - which no longer has a roof at all!

WHY TUNNELS WERE DUG

One of the biggest problems to canal builders was, and is, the requirement of a level 'pound' of water over several miles. Unfortunately most of Great Britain is not flat!

The canal would twist and wind round hillsides as much as possible; locks would be used if necessary to raise the canal to the level of the terrain on its course. Often the canal would reach either an outcrop of rock which was difficult to get round, or a hill that could not easily be surmounted by locks. Tunnels were then the only remaining option, constructed almost as a means of last resort. Before embarking upon the building of a tunnel, the surveyors and engineers would consider the following alternatives:

▲ *Blisworth – south portal*

LOCKS
The use of locks to raise the canal up and over a hill required vast amounts of water. It was often the case that a good supply of water was not available at the summit level to feed such locks. Locks would be used only as necessary to raise or lower the canal to a new level.

CUTTINGS
Deep cuttings were often discounted on the grounds that they were too difficult or too costly. Moving thousands of tons of material was extremely time-consuming, especially with the available equipment; picks, shovels and black powder. Lack of expertise in matters of ground stability often lead to banks collapsing or wash ins, following a downpour.

LIFTS & INCLINED PLANES
The construction of inclined planes, and other mechanical devices such as lifts were only suitable for moving cargo from one level to another within a controlled area such as a colliery. Although a few of these devices were built, most were soon superseded and abandoned

THE ENORMITY OF THE TASK

The decision to construct a tunnel was not the end of the problem. Tunnels were often very difficult to build. They invariably took longer, and cost far more than planned. The tunnels were often the first parts of a canal project to be started, but often the last to be finished. Many canals which were otherwise complete could only be used in part until their tunnels were finished. A typical example is Blisworth, which was started when the Grand Junction canal was given approval in 1793, but abandoned after three years of construction due to geological problems. The replacement followed a different line, but was not opened until 1805, some years after the rest of the canal was navigable and in use.

The methods of tunnel construction were in their infancy when the first canals were built. The only similar engineering experience came from mining. Routes were influenced by many factors, not all of a technical nature. The geology of the hill was often unknown, making the whole project a risk. Workings had often to be abandoned and modified due to poor rock and soil, problems with water and geological faults. Rock and soil problems led to some tunnels collapsing whilst being dug, others had to be abandoned due to excess water and flooding. Given all these hidden problems, and the basic methods of construction, it is surprising that most tunnels finished up reasonably straight, and many remain open over two hundred years later.

CONSTRUCTION

Construction was dangerous and difficult. Rock and stone was removed using black powder, picks and shovels. The planned length of the tunnel determined whether construction was to be by cutting through from either end (usually less than 300 yards), or by digging shafts. These shafts were joined to each other at the bottom by a series of tunnels which were then opened out. This method allowed more men to work at the same time, thus speeding up excavation. Some longer tunnels had as many as twenty-five shafts, thereby creating fifty-two faces for digging. As many as three hundred men would sometimes be engaged to work on a tunnel for months or even years.

STAGE 1

A line of stakes would be driven into the ground in a straight line, over the hill, following the proposed route of the tunnel. The land was surveyed to determine how deep each shaft would need to be dug, in order that their bases could all be joined at the same level.

STAGE 2

Shafts would be dug from the top of the hill down to the proposed canal level. As the shafts deepened they would be lined with brick, in the manner of mine shafts.

The shafts proved to be an important aid to construction, providing a means by which spoil could be removed from the workings. The spoil was either carried away to be used in the construction of embankments, or simply dumped at the top of the shafts. In some cases valuable minerals including coal would be sold to subsidise costs.

The shafts provided ventilation to the workings, many being left to perform the same function for the tunnel once completed.

STAGE 3

A system for removing spoil and bringing in bricks and mortar was set up as the vertical and the end shafts progressed. Winches were erected above the shafts to lift the spoil in buckets. The only way to remove spoil in bulk was by horse and cart. As most tunnels were constructed with a bore of over 12ft, it was necessary to use large quantities of timber as shoring and elementary scaffolding. This added to the logistical problems involved. On longer tunnels, as the work progressed tracks were often installed along the dry canal bed to allow spoil to be removed by means of a train of small trucks.

STAGE 4

When the shaft had reached the required depth, the mouth was bisected on the surface by a rod following the original surveyed path (set out in stage 1). Plumb lines were then fixed and dropped into the shaft. At the bottom of the shaft, the plumb lines were immersed in water or mercury to keep them steady. The joining of the two lines gave the direction in which the tunnel should be dug on either side of the shaft. Horses were used to drive a 'horse-gin' (a type of winch), which would lift the buckets containing the spoil to the surface.

STAGE 5

Each of the shafts were joined in turn enabling the line of the tunnel to be checked. When all the shafts had been joined and met by the workings dug from the both entrances, an embryonic small bore tunnel had been created.

The embryonic tunnel was then dug out to its full bore, and lined where necessary with brick over a wooden framework. Clay was usually rammed behind this structure to fill the space between the rock in an attempt to provide a waterproof lining. Above the waterline measures were taken to allow groundwater to drain out of the surrounding rock, thus relieving pressure on the brick lining. In Sapperton tunnel, for example, the section that finally collapsed was found to have insufficient relief holes. This deficiency resulted in unbearable pressure on the brickwork holding back the indiginous Fullers Earth.

There are examples of tunnels which are not lined such as Cowley and Dunsley, the jagged walls and roof being formed out of the rock.

VENTS

▲ *A Netherton vent*

When visiting tunnels, the remaining shafts can be used as a guide to the line of the canal under the ground. Longer tunnels had many shafts; for example Blisworth had nineteen, of which only ten remain as ventilation, the others being capped.

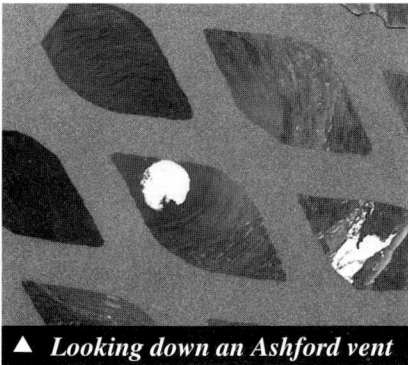

▲ *Looking down an Ashford vent*

Many of the shafts were filled in or capped with only a few being left for ventilation. Those that were left were often built up some ten to fifteen feet or more proud of the ground. The purpose of such constructions (examples exist at Netherton, Gosty Hill and Standedge) was to stop people falling in, or vandals throwing things down into the canal below.

Some vents have a simple grating over them at ground level beside the horse path. An example of this can be found at Ashford tunnel, where the opening enables you to see boats pass beneath or see your reflection in the water.

PORTALS

Portals were built at either end. Many were simple structures such as those found on the Trent and Mersey at Barnton, Preston Brook and Saltersford, or very ornate as at Bath or Sapperton.

▲ *Barnton – south portal*

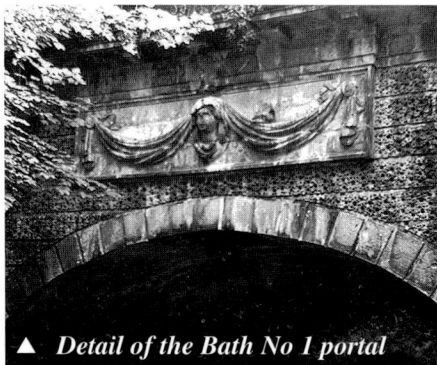

▲ *Detail of the Bath No 1 portal*

On some portals, the indvidual mason took the opportunity to leave their personal marks, as can be seen on the tunnels on the Leeds & Liverpool canal, at Foulridge and Gannow.

ALTERATIONS & IMPROVEMENTS

The first tunnels had a bore which was only slightly wider than the maximum beam allowed by the bridges and locks constructed elsewhere on the canal. They had no tow paths which meant the horses had to be lead over the top. Being only a single bore, the first tunnels allowed only single working, which caused bottlenecks and delays.

Once the tunnel was opened, the problems did not cease. Subsidence, collapses, and bottle necks were, and remain, the main problems. Some tunnels have been modified to alleviate the problems. For example Fenny Compton was once one tunnel. It was divided into two to provide a passing point to reduce bottlenecks, and then finally opened out altogether. Bottleneck problems warranted the digging of a second tunnel at Harecastle. Subsequent subsidence has seen the closing of the original tunnel leaving the second open for navigation. The second tunnel has been modified with the removal of its once integral tow path.

With the construction of more and more canals, experience of building tunnels grew. Tunnels were built with wider bores enabling two boats to pass, and longer, more ambitious projects were attempted. Given the methods of construction, and the number still open to navigation, the tunnels are a testimony to the ingenuity and skill of the engineers and workmen who planned and built them so many years ago.

The Engineers

Dunhampstead tunnel

THE DUKE OF BRIDGEWATER
1736 – 1803

Francis Egerton, the third Duke of Bridgewater is recorded by history as the father of British inland navigation. Many early influences may have been responsible for his enthusiasm for water transport; not least his father, the first Duke, who was instrumental in improving waterway navigation on the River Weaver.

Through his land agent John Gilbert, and Gilbert's brother Thomas, Bridgewater was introduced to the remarkable James Brindley. Their collaboration began in 1759 and resulted in the first true canal in England. The Bridgewater canal was eventually forty-two miles long and initially connected Worsley with Manchester. The stretch opened in 1761. It eventually brought Bridgewater huge profits from coal sales and haulage, which encouraged entrepreneurs such as Josiah Wedgewood to start similar canal schemes.

The Duke's eccentricities and rough language endeared him to his canal workers, but frequently offended polite society. It was said he rarely washed and wore the same brown suit for weeks until both he and it stank to high heaven! However, he was undoubtedly a shrewd man; he viewed the coming of the railways with suspicion, observing prophetically 'I see mischief in those damned tramways'.

JAMES BRINDLEY
1716 – 1772

A crofter's son, born near Chapel-en-le-Firth, Derbyshire, Brindley was was apprenticed to a millwright before setting up on his own in Leek, Staffordshire. He soon showed his talent as an engineer; in 1752 he designed a water-driven engine for draining coalmines, and followed this by conceiving a revolutionary silk mill. Brindley's extraordinary achievements brought him to the attention of the Duke of Bridgewater. In 1759, Bridgewater commissioned his land agent John Gilbert and Brindley to build a canal linking Worsley with Manchester. Like almost every other project Brindley participated in, the canal proved a triumph.

Now enjoying a national reputation, Brindley went on to construct over 365 miles of canal, including the Birmingham and Oxford canals, and the initial stages of the Grand Trunk canal. Amazingly, Brindley was illiterate and rarely used technical drawings. He tended to resolve particularly difficult engineering problems by taking to bed. Apparently, the solution almost always emerged after a period of sleep! Despite delegating much work to assistants, Brindley's health suffered badly from overwork. This stress, together with the afflications of diabetes and nephritis contracted whilst surveying did not help his health. His demise came whilst surveying the line of the future Caldon canal, when he was soaked in a downpour and caught a chill. Brindley died soon after, on 27 September 1772. His brother-in-law, Hugh Henshall took over his commitments on the Trent & Mersey and Chesterfield canals. Apart from the surviving examples of his civil engineering, the memory of this famous pioneer of inland navigation is now commemorated by the *James Brindley* pub, which stands by Gas Street Basin on the Birmingham Canal Navigation.

THOMAS CARTWRIGHT
Died 1810

Cartwright was engaged as chief engineer of the Worcester & Birmingham canal between 1791 and 1801. During this time he supervised the construction of the tunnel at Edgbaston and Wast Hill tunnel at King's Norton. His tenure came to a close as the Worcester & Birmingham suffered from serious financial difficulties and embezzlement by its treasurer.

Cartwright did not want for work elsewhere, however, and immediately switched his attention to Wales, where he had replaced Thomas Dadford junior as chief engineer of the Brecknock & Abergavenny.

When work resumed on the Worcester & Birmingham canal in 1805, Thomas Cartwright was re-enaged and forged onwards towards Worcester, completing Shortwood tunnel and begining work at Tardebigge.

Cartwright was probably showing signs of illness by 1809, when he was replaced as chief engineer of the Worcester & Birmingham by John Woodhouse. At the same time, William Crossley took over Cartwright's duties on the Brecknock & Abergavenny. Cartwright died in 1810, the year Tardebigge tunnel was completed.

Thomas Cartwright's son, William, followed in his father's footsteps as a canal engineer, working on the Lancaster canal as resident under John Rennie.

JOSIAH CLOWES
Circa 1736 – 1795

Josiah Clowes was a Cheshire man, born at Middlewich. He began his career in civil engineering around 1775, as a contractor on the Trent & Mersey canal. Advancement came with an appointment as chief engineer of the Chester canal, but he was ignominiously sacked in 1778.

In 1783, working hard to regain his reputation, Clowes accepted a position as resident engineer to Robert Whitworth on the Thames & Severn. Whitworth gave him particular responsibility for the construction of Sapperton tunnel. Clowes completed Sapperton, one of the longest tunnels ever attempted, in 1789, and suddenly found his services in great demand. Later that year, he moved up to the Midlands to take over the difficult project of Dudley tunnel. Dudley had already proved too much for Thomas Dadford senior and John Pinkerton, but with his confidence bolstered by his recent triumph, Clowes turned the project around and completed the tunnel in 1792.

By now firmly established as one of the leading canal engineers in the country, Clowes obtained several other appointments, such as chief engineer of the Hereford & Gloucester canal. He went on to design Berwick tunnel on the Shrewsbury canal, as well as the original Longdon aqueduct. Clowes died in 1795, before Berwick was completed, and his place was taken by the famous Thomas Telford. It is a measure of the enormous pressure success had brought on Josiah Clowes that other projects in progress at his death included the canal tunnels at Brandwood, Gosty Hill, Lapal and Oxenhall.

WILLIAM CROSSLEY

Active circa 1799 – 1831

Crossley followed his father's profession as a canal engineer, and presumably gained his early experience (and business contacts) under the elder William's tutelage.

The son's first prominent position came when he was appointed resident engineer of the Rochdale canal, under William Jessop. He had a hand in the tunnel at Deansgate.

In 1809 Crossley moved on to an appointment on the Brecknock & Abergavenny, and held this until 1811, at which time he was promoted to replace the late Thomas Cartwright as chief engineer . Despite problems in constructing the aqueduct at Pontymoile, the canal was complete by 1813. Cartwright's other important appointment, on the Worcester & Birmingham, had gone to John Woodhouse. Eventually, however, Woodhouse's employers became disenchanted with him, and brought in Crossley as a replacement. Woodhouse stayed on as a contractor, but technically Crossley was the chief engineer when Dunhampstead was completed in 1815.

As a resident engineer of the Lancaster canal under John Rennie, Crossley gained considerable profit from his success as the supervisor of Hincaster tunnel, finished in 1817. After Hincaster was opened, Crossley was kept hard at work assessing the feasibility of various branch lines . Following considerable surveys of various routes, work began on the Glasson branch (linking the Lancaster canal to the sea) in 1823 and opened in 1825. By this time Crossley's part in the successful completion of the Hincaster project had resulted in his appointment as superintendent of the Lancaster canal. In 1826 William Crossley was appointed chief engineer of the Macclesfield canal, which he brought to completion in 1831.

SIR WILLIAM CUBITT

1785 – 1861

William Cubitt was born at Dilham in Norfolk. He began his working life as a miller, then turned his hand to cabinet making, before becoming a millwright. In 1807 Cubitt came to public notice when he patented a new design for windmill sails. Five years later he was appointed chief engineer at Robert Ransome's Orwell Works in Ipswich, and rose to become a partner in the Suffolk business by 1821. Two years later Cubitt moved to London and began to establish a national reputation.

Displaying the easy confidence so typical of the Victorian entrepreneur, Cubitt moved smoothly into the field of canal engineering. His main contribution to inland navigation was the rationalisation of the Oxford canal between Braunston and Hawkesbury. Having surveyed the meandering route of Brindley's original canal, Cubitt cut a new straight course, discarding fourteen miles of waterway, and the existing tunnels at Newbold and Wolfhampcote. In 1834, in place of Brindley's original tunnel at Newbold, Cubitt's designed a more modern construction with a double towpath.

During the 1830s the engineer was engaged on various projects up and down the country, bringing the Victorian obsession of 'improvement' to the ageing canal network. In 1833, he was called in to aid, and then replace, the ageing Thomas Telford as chief engineer of the Birmingham & Liverpool Junction canal. In July 1835 Cubitt was able to report that he had completed the troubled project and saved the canal company into the bargain. Apart from his work on Britain's waterways, Cubitt worked on the Southeastern Railway, and also designed the Bute Docks in Cardiff as well as Berlin's waterworks. In 1851 he was involved in the construction of buildings for Prince Albert's Great Exhibition. Knighted for his services to the country, Sir William Cubitt served as Lord Mayor of London from 1860 to 1861. His name lives on in Cubitt Town, on the Isle of Dogs in Greater London.

THOMAS DADFORD JNR.
Died 1806

As the eldest son of the experienced and well-connected civil engineer Thomas Dadford, it is not surprising that Thomas Dadford junior held a succession of high profile appointments on the canal network.

Dadford junior worked on the Stourbridge canal from 1776 until 1787, gaining tunnelling experience at Brettell Lane, before becoming surveyor and engineer of the Leominster canal. The ill-fated Leominster canal involved tunnels at Newnham, Pensax, Putnal Fields and Southnet - although the waterway was never completed and Southnet collapsed. Dadford must bear his share of responsibility for the Leominster's problems; certainly John Rennie thought so, as his report on the canal was highly critical of the design of Dadford's tunnels, particularly Newnham.

He was jointly chief engineer and contractor with his father, Thomas Dadford senior, on the Glamorganshire canal. Around the time the Dadfords were supervising work on Cardiff tunnel, they and a partner, Thomas Sheasby, were arrested for alleged breach of contract. At a board of inquiry, Robert Whitworth accepted their claims that it was the company who were in the wrong and the Dadfords were vindicated.

The younger Dadford stayed in Wales for the remainder of his career in Britain. He was chief engineer of the Neath canal in 1791, and accepted a similar appointment on the Monmouthshire canal in 1792. He helped his brother John on the Montgomeryshire canal between 1794 and 1797. Tunnels on the Welsh canals which owe their existence to Dadford junior include Ashford, Cwmbran and Newport. At the turn of the century Thomas Dadford emigrated to America, where he died in 1806.

THOMAS DADFORD SNR.
Died 1809

Dadford first came to notice as an assistant of James Brindley, working alongside colleagues such as Samuel Simcock on the Staffordshire & Worcestershire canal. He was resident engineer at Cookley and Dunsley, which were completed around 1770.

As a protege of the famous Brindley, Dadford was a natural choice to supervise the Dudley tunnel project on the Dudley No. 1 canal, but, defeated by the problems, he was dismissed along with the contractor John Pinkerton, in 1787. This humiliation clearly had a detrimental effect on Dadford's career, for he was forced to tender for work as a mere cutting contractor for William Jessop on the Cromford canal. However, Dadford's reputation appears to have revived somewhat, for he and Benjamin Outram are listed as Jessop's assistants at Butterley and Gregory.

Fortune continued to smile on Dadford when he was appointed joint engineer and contractor with his son and namesake, Thomas Dadford junior, on the Glamorganshire canal. However, drama was to follow in 1794 when the Glamorganshire canal company had the Dadfords and their partner Thomas Sheasby arrested for breach of contract (around the time they were engaged on a tunnel at Cardiff). The Dadfords fought back, claiming that they had withheld their work because the company owed them a considerable sum of arrears. Robert Whitworth was called in to head an inquiry into the matter, and exonerated the engineers.

Thomas Dadford's final appointment was to the Montgomeryshire canal, where he succeeded another of his sons, John Dadford, as chief engineer. A third son, James, acted as chief engineer of the Gloucestershire & Berkeley canal from 1797 to 1800.

MATTHEW FLETCHER
1731 – 1801

As the son of a Bolton mine owner, Matthew Fletcher's early career had been spent as a mining engineer. It was because of his mining interests that he became involved with a proposal that would result in the Manchester, Bolton & Bury canal.

Fletcher, a committee member of the Manchester, Bolton & Bury Company, surveyed the putative route in 1790, and proceeded to take an active part in its construction. The canal required a two-part tunnel at Bury. As overall supervisor Fletcher worked alongside Charles Roberts, but eventually replaced this engineer with his own nephew, John Nightingale.

In 1799, Matthew Fletcher angered fellow committee members of the Manchester, Bolton & Bury when he became chairman of a rival scheme, and immediately conspired to defeat legislation designed to extend the Manchester, Bolton & Bury. Fletcher was subsequently ousted from the management of the canal.

Despite his acrimonious parting with the Manchester, Bolton & Bury, other companies found Fletcher's mining experience extremely useful. One such concern was the Huddersfield canal company, who employed him as a consultant on their preliminary work at Standedge tunnel.

JOHN GILBERT
1724 – 1795

With his brother Thomas, John Gilbert can be ranked among the greatest influences on the development of British inland waterways. The brothers were the sons of a minor landowner in Cotton, near Alton in Staffordshire. John Gilbert, the younger son, was apprenticed to the famous Matthew Boulton, and gained his early experience at Boulton's works based at Soho, Birmingham.

Gilbert became land agent to the third Duke of Bridgewater at Worsley, his appointment no doubt helped by his engineering background. He used his practical experience to extend and improve the drainage system at the Duke's mines, before, with his brother, beginning an involvement with canal navigation.

Through Thomas, the Duke of Bridgewater was introduced to the remarkable James Brindley. A collaboration began in 1759, with John Gilbert as supervisor of the project which would result in the first true canal in England: the Bridgewater canal. The stretch opened in 1761, and eventually brought Bridgewater huge profits from coal sales and haulage. The success of the waterway opened the eyes of other entrepreneurs such as Josiah Wedgwood in the Potteries, and many canal schemes began to spring up across the country. Gilbert's involvement in this revolution has been somewhat under-estimated, and it is now known that he played a far greater part in the actual design and construction than was previously realised. He can be credited with some of the success of the tunnels at Worsley, and went on to supervise the construction of Hughes Bridge tunnel, in partnership with his brother. John Gilbert's memory is today preserved in a very practical way in the pub at Worsley which bears his name.

THOMAS GILBERT MP
1720 – 1816

Thomas Gilbert, the elder son of a Staffordshire landowner, trained as a lawyer in London. He became land agent to Lord Gower, whose ancestors had been important figures in Staffordshire and Shropshire for generations. During his duties, which included work on improving navigation of the Trent, Thomas became friendly with a talented local craftsman, by the name of James Brindley.

John, Thomas' younger brother, acted as land agent for Lord Gower's brother-in-law, the Duke of Bridgewater, who was always looking for ways to improve his coal-mining interests and navigation on his estates. In 1759 Thomas famously introduced the Duke to Brindley. The meeting of these two men from very different backgrounds, together with the largely unsung contribution of John Gilbert, facilitated the most famous partnership in the history of British inland navigation.

Thomas and his brother continued to be notable sponsors of canal development and were major subscribers to both the Shropshire and Shrewsbury canal.

Thomas Gilbert eventually entered Parliament as an MP, and gained a reputation as a Parliamentary reformer. The Poor Law Act of 1752 was named "Gilbert's Act" in recognition of his energetic involvement in its passage through Parliament.

HUGH HENSHALL
Circa 1734 – 1816

Hugh Henshall's father was a land surveyor, and a close friend of James Brindley. Brindley took the young Henshall under his wing and trained him as his principal assistant. Later, although Brindley was of advanced years, he took Henshall's nineteen year old sister as his wife and the alliance between the two families was sealed.

Henshall took over most of his brother-in-law's obligations when Brindley died in 1772, most particularly the Trent & Mersey and the Chesterfield canals. As Brindley had rather over-extended himself, it was hardly surprising that some contractors and even some resident engineers had taken advantage of the lack of close supervision. Henshall was particularly critical of the workmanship he found on the Chesterfield canal in the summer of 1773. However, the shortcomings were rectified and the canal, together with the tunnels at Norwood and Drakeholes, was completed in 1775.

A number of projects similarly required completion on the Trent & Mersey, including the tunnels at Barnton, Preston Brook, Saltersford and Harecastle. Henshall also carried on Brindley's work on the adjoining Caldon canal; he was actually responsible for the low tunnel at Froghall sometimes erroneously attributed to John Rennie.

Henshall eventually emerged from Brindley's shadow with his work on the Hereford & Gloucester in 1791. He then acted as a consultant to the Manchester, Bolton & Bury canal, advising Matthew Fletcher on operations at Bury. By the end of his life, Hugh Henshall's portfolio had expanded to include railway engineering, most notably the Great Western line.

WILLIAM JESSOP
1745 – 1814

The son of a Devonport shipwright, William Jessop has been described as 'the greatest canal engineer of the age'. At the age of 16 he became a pupil of the civil engineer John Smeaton, and served his apprenticeship on canals in Yorkshire. In 1773 Jessop accompanied his mentor to work on the Grand Canal near Dublin.

Jessop was soon much in demand as a surveyor of new canal projects such as the Trent (1783), Staffs and Worcs (1784) and the Flint Coal canal (1785). His cost estimates usually included a shrewd analysis of local trade conditions, although a financial entanglement over the Birmingham canal project in 1787 proved that his judgement was not always perfect.

An energetic entrepreneur with a wide range of interests, in 1790 Jessop and his partner Benjamin Outram founded the Butterley Ironworks - a concern which is still in production over two centuries later. The fish-bellied cast-iron rails developed and produced at Butterley proved to be a great advance in rail track technology. Over the next two decades Jessop was to supervise the construction of the Surrey Iron Railway, Bristol's Avon Docks and the huge West India Docks in the Port of London.

Like Smeaton, Jessop had a noted preference for wide canals, not least because of the need to link up with coastal and sea-going trade. Jessop in his turn became a mentor of Thomas Telford, who first became an employee in 1797 and worked under Jessop in the construction of the Pontcysyllte aqueduct (Ellesmere canal 1805). Jessop is best remembered as chief engineer of the Grand Junction canal with its spectacular tunnel at Blisworth. His son, Josias Jessop, was also a notable civil engineer.

BENJAMIN OUTRAM
1764 – 1805

Benjamin Outram, of Alfreton in Derbyshire, was named after Benjamin Franklin, a friend of the Outram family. He trained as an engineer, and became particularly well known for his tramroads. It is often said that 'trams' were named after Outram, but in fact the term originally applied to planks used on the early railroads.

Around 1799 Outram, in partnership with William Jessop, founded the Butterley Ironworks. This huge site still manufactures metal goods from its base near Butterley tunnel.

Outram gained experience of civil engineering when he assisted Jessop on the Cromford canal, with its tunnels at Butterley, Gregory, Hag and Buckland Hollow. He subsequently became chief engineer of the Peak Forest canal, an appointment not without problems as his position was initially undermined by a contractor, Robert Fulton. Outram "a fine-looking, high-spirited man, of a generous temper and restless energy" did not suffer foolish employers glady, and "could brook neither stupidity or opposition" from subordinates. The chief engineer prevailed over his ambitious assistant and must therefore take most of the credit for Hyde Bank, Rose Hill and Woodley tunnels.

Outram began work on the Huddersfield Narrow canal, with its famous tunnel at Standedge, but fell ill and had to be replaced by Robert Whitworth. Outram's fame has been over-shadowed by the exploits of his son, General Sir James Outram (1803-1863), a renowned military commander who commanded the defence of Lucknow during the Indian Mutiny of 1857.

JOHN PINKERTON
Died 1803

The name of Pinkerton is perhaps one of the most notorious in the history of canal tunnel construction, although whether his infamy is deserved or not is a frequently argued subject. Pinkerton appears to have been a Yorkshireman, hailing from the West Riding. With his brother, James, he first appeared as a contractor on the Driffield Navigation in 1768, then again on the Market Weighton canal some four years later.

The Pinkerton brothers became associates of William Jessop, working on the Selby canal between 1775 and 1778, then on the Erewash until 1779. John Pinkerton then went back north to perform contract work on the Calder & Hebble.

By 1783 the brothers, again in partnership, found themselves in work on the Trent. Jessop secured them further contracts at Dudley tunnel in 1785. This lucrative employment lasted until 1787, when John Pinkerton was dismissed. A reputation for drunkeness and sloppy workmanship began to stick to John in particular, for having secured another contract on the Birmingham & Fazeley canal, he found himself sacked yet again in 1789. However, Pinkerton's work for John Smeaton's tunnel at Curdworth appears to have been reasonably sound.

Smeaton's protege William Jessop kept faith with John Pinkerton, despite growing evidence of his incompetence. The engineer may have revised his opinion when Pinkerton's work on the Basingstoke canal, including the Greywell tunnel completed around 1794, was again said to have fallen below the standards required. Undeterred, John Pinkerton continued to obtain construction contracts, ending his career on the Gloucester & Berkeley. James Pinkerton was later engineer of the Kidwelly & Llanelly canal.

JOHN RENNIE
1761 – 1821

John Rennie, an energetic giant standing 6'4" in height, must have cut an imposing figure on the canals. Rennie was born in 1761 at Phantassie Farm, East Linton, Scotland, the fourth son of a wealthy farmer. Like James Brindley, he began his working life as a millwright. Rennie was apprenticed to Andrew Meikle at the age of 12, but, showing great aptitude for mathematics, entered Edinburgh University in 1780.

On his graduation from Edinburgh in 1783, Rennie entered employment with the famous engineering company Boulton and Watt. In 1791 he set up on his own as an engineer. The gamble was successful, and Rennie soon acquired a reputation as a highly competent bridge-builder. Examples of his work include Kelso, Leeds, Musselburgh, old Southwark and Waterloo Bridge in London. Rennie also supervised renovation, and in some cases complete rebuilding of many docks and harbours in England and Scotland.

Rennie's importance to inland navigation was scarcely less than his other feats of civil engineering. The young Scot began work on the Lancaster canal in 1793, and in 1802 took over from Hugh Henshall on the Caldon canal His involvement with the Caldon was to last almost twenty years and produced the tunnels at Leek (1802) and Alton (1819). As his fame grew, Rennie accepted appointments on several other canals which competed for his time. He was the engineer responsible for the Basingstoke (1794), and for the Kennet & Avon (1810). As chief engineer of the Lancaster canal, he bore the ultimate responsibility for Whittle Hills (1804) and Hincaster (finally finished in1817).

The prestigious project of London Bridge was to have been the crowning point of John Rennie's career, but he died in 1821 whilst the project was still in its planning stage. Rennie was laid to rest in the crypt of St Paul's Cathedral. London Bridge was completed ten years later by his son, Sir John Rennie (1794-1874).

WILLIAM REYNOLDS
1758 – 1803

William was the son of Richard Reynolds, a Bristol iron merchant, and a cousin of the Darby family in Coalbrookdale. His interest in canals grew from concern to improve the profitability of his family's mining and metalworking centres.

An ambitious project centured around the Coal Tar tunnel at Blists Hill (in modern day Telford) was begun in 1786, designed to provide access to the Severn. However, work was curtailed when the surrounding geology was found to be full of seeping bitumen.

Reynolds's confidence was clearly unshaken by this reverse, for further private work included his own Ketley canal, with the tunnel at Ketley completed around 1797.

William Reynolds went on to complete the Wombridge canal, and subscribed to the larger project of the Shrewsbury canal. He took a very active interest in his investment, and at times acted as a supervisor of work on the canal itself. He participated in the construction of Berwick tunnel, completed in 1796, with a raised wooden towpath made to his design.

JOHN SMEATON
1724 – 1794

John Smeaton was a Yorkshireman, born in a village near Leeds in 1724. His early education was in the law, but he gave up his studies and became an instrument maker. He moved to London around 1750 and soon gained recognition for his many talents.

Smeaton was elected a Fellow of the Royal Society in 1753 and awarded the Copley Medal for his design work with waterwheels and windmills. From 1756 to 1759 he supervised the construction of the third Eddystone lighthouse. This remarkable construction remained in service until 1877, when it was taken down and re-erected on Plymouth Hoe. Smeaton followed this triumph by improving steam engine technology and building canals.

In 1761 Smeaton took on a young William Jessop as his apprentice. Smeaton trained Jessop on canals in England before taking him to Ireland in 1773 to work on the Grand Canal at Dublin. In the midst of his commitments on Britain's waterways, Smeaton found time to construct Ramsgate Harbour in 1774. He then took up appointments in Scotland, on the Forth & Clyde canal, and built bridges at Coldsteam and Perth.

Smeaton's most enduring momument on the British waterways network is possibly Curdworth tunnel on the Birmingham & Fazeley canal. This was completed in 1789, just five years before his death at the age of seventy. Smeaton's funeral memorial in Yorkshire, features a bas relief of Eddystone lighthouse - perhaps his greatest achievement.

THOMAS TELFORD
1757 – 1834

Thomas Telford was a shepherd's son, born in Westerkirk, near Langholm in Scotland. He was apprenticed to a local stonemason at the age of fourteen, but after he had served his apprenticeship moved on to Edinburgh, and then London. By 1784 he was working at Portsmouth dockyard, and three years later he was appointed surveyor of public works for the county of Shropshire.

The construction of a spectacular bridge over the Severn at Montford (1790-92) brought him to the notice of other professionals, followed by the Pontcysylte aqueduct and other works on the Ellesmere canal between 1793 and 1805. By this time he had effectively taken over from William Jessop on the Llangollen canal, and with Thomas Denson supervised the completion of the tunnels at Chirk and Whitehouses (1802). He also had a significant role in the construction of Ellesmere.

The following year he was given a commission by the government to survey various public works in Scotland, and constructed the Caledonian canal between 1803 and 1823. At the same time he designed and supervised the famous Menai suspension bridge (1819-26) and St Katherine's Docks in London (1824-28). In 1825 he began a programme of improvement to the Birmingham Canal Navigations, which lasted until 1838. During this time he constructed at Galton a bridge which featured the then largest bridge span in the world.

The most famous of Telford's canal tunnels continues to be Harecastle II on the Trent & Mersey canal, completed in 1827. In contrast to the time involved in Brindley's original Harecastle I, Telford's tunnel took only two years to complete. By the end of his long life, besides his contibution to the British canal network, Telford had been responsible for the construction of 1,000 miles of road as well as 1,200 bridges and public works. The Shropshire new town of Telford is named after him.

ROBERT WHITWORTH
Died 1799

Robert Whitworth began his training under James Brindley. As one of Brindley's principal assistants, the young man surveyed the original line of the Oxford canal in 1768. He went on to work on the Coventry canal, and acted as a consultant on several more, including the proposed line of the future Leeds & Liverpool.

Whitworth acquired a reputation as a troubleshooter, producing crisis reports on the Herefordshire & Gloucestershire and the Leominster canals. He arbitrated a dispute between the Dadfords and the Glamorganshire canal company, exonerating the engineers who had been arrested for breach of contract. Although surveyor and engineer of the Thames & Severn canal, Whitworth left more and more of the day-to-day running to his assistant, Josiah Clowes. Sapperton tunnel, technically under Whitworth's direction, was essentially Clowes' work.

In 1789, Whitworth was engaged as a consultant by the Leeds & Liverpool canal company, and first proposed a tunnel at Foulridge. He became chief engineer of the canal in 1790, with his son Robert as his assistant. Like many of his peers, Whitworth rather over-stretched himself with commitments all over the country, but took on the supervision of the Herefordshire & Gloucestershire canal, when his former assistant Josiah Clowes died in 1795. His tenure saw Oxenhall tunnel completed.

In 1792, Robert Whitworth and his son were also appointed joint engineers of the Ashby canal. Their employers became increasingly intolerant of the Whitworths' frequent absence, and, although work at Snarestone tunnel was under way, the pair were dismissed in 1797. The episode did not appear to harm Whitworth's reputation; when Benjamin Outram was incapacitated by illness, the Huddersfield canal company brought him in to help complete Scout tunnel. Ironically Outram survived Whitworth, who died with his final tunnel project (Gannow) unfinished on the Leeds & Liverpool canal.

JOHN WOODHOUSE
Active 1805 – 1820

John Woodhouse, a native of Ashby-de-la-Zouch, first came to notice as a contractor on the Grand Junction canal. He worked on Blisworth tunnel, but the project possibly bankrupted him. Consequently, Woodhouse accepted a rather humbler position as a staff engineer on the Grand Junction, serving from 1805 to 1809.

Thomas Cartwright, chief engineer of the Worcester & Birmingham, was seriously ill by 1809 and unfit for work. Woodhouse, who had come to the notice of the company with an experimental lift at Tardebigge two years before, was brought in as his replacement. He finished Cartwright's design at Tardebigge tunnel in 1810. Although the lift worked perfectly, the canal company and their consultant John Rennie were unconvinced and Woodhouse was instructed to dismantle it and begin work on the famous Tardebigge flight of locks.

The Worcester & Birmingham canal were obviously exacting employers, and eventually replaced their chief engineer with William Crossley. John Woodhouse continued an association with the Worcester & Birmingham, however, as a contractor, until around 1815. He had a large part in the construction of Dunhamstead.

Woodhouse's topsy-turvy career again appeared to have revived when he was appointed resident engineer of the Gloucestershire & Berkeley - but he was sacked by Thomas Telford when the Scotsman discovered that Woodhouse and his son were defrauding the company by supplying sub-standard stone whilst charging premium rates.

The Tunnels

TUNNEL LENGTHS

Few subjects excite as much debate and passion in canal enthusiasts as the true length of this or that tunnel. A recent letter to a canal magazine listed six different lengths for Norwood tunnel alone!

The main problem is that there is no one ideal, objective method of measurement which would resolve the question of length in every case. Ideally, one would traverse the tunnel and measure it - except that this is not possible in the case of tunnels which have collapsed or disappeared. The fact that even working tunnels have kinks and bends presents a problem for those who would use laser technology, or theodolites, or measure Ordinance Survey maps. Neither would trawling through the archives or original engineering drawings necessarily help - as many tunnels deviated from the plans or were subsequently altered.

The list below, therefore, represents our best guess - gleaned from comparing previously published measurements, reading engineering plans and gathering information on-site - at the relative length of canal tunnels in England and Wales. We have also tried to separate out anomalies such as Pensax, which although never completed was a very long tunnel only exceeded by Standedge and Strood.

Tunnel	Length	Date	Page	Alternative names (*in italics*) & other comments
Standedge	5,210 m (5,698 yd)	1811	p.112	*Marsden*
Strood	3,608 m (3,946 yd)	1824	p.114	*Higham.* Now railway tunnel.
Sapperton	3,490 m (3,817 yd)	1789	p.103	Largest volume
Lapal	3,470 m (3,795 yd)	1798	p.88	Collapsed
Dudley	2,884 m (3,154 yd)	1792	p.66	Calculated portal to portal
Norwood	2,836 m (3,102 yd)	1775	p.95	Collapsed
Butterley	2,801 m (3,063 yd)	1794	p.51	
Blisworth	2,794 m (3,056 yd)	1805	p.43	
Netherton	2,768 m (3,027 yd)	1858	p.91	Double towpath
Harecastle II	2,676 m (2,926 yd)	1827	p.83	
Harecastle I	2,633 m (2,879 yd)	1777	p.82	Closed 1918
Wast Hill	2,493 m (2,726 yd)	1797	p.117	*King's Norton, West Hill.*
Morwelldown	2,322 m (2,540 yd)	1814	p.90	*Morwellham*
Oxenhall	2,004 m (2,192 yd)	c.1798	p.97	Collapsed
Braunston	1,867 m (2,042 yd)	1796	p.45	
Crimson Hill	1,646 m (1,800 yd)	1839	p.60	Closed
Foulridge	1,500 m (1,640 yd)	1796	p.73	
Crick	1,397 m (1,528 yd)	1814	p.58	
Southnet	1,146 m (1,254 yd)	1795	p.110	Never connected to its parent canal
Preston Brook	1,136 m (1,242 yd)	1775	p.98	
Greywell	1,125 m (1,230 yd)	1794	p.80	Collapsed 1932. Now a designated SSSI
Husbands Bosworth	1,066 m (1,166 yd)	1813	p.85	
Berwick	887 m (970 yd)	1796	p.42	*Preston*
Islington	878 m (960 yd)	1818	p.87	*Hell*
Fenny Compton	862 m (943 yd)	1778	p.72	Opened up - with a gap for some years
Saddington	805 m (880 yd)	1797	p.101	

Tunnel	Length			Date	Page	Alternative names (*in italics*) & other comments
Shortwood	561 m (	613 yd)		1807	p.106	
Eardington	549 m (	600 yd)		1792	p.68	Closed 1889
Tardebigge	530 m (	580 yd)		1810	p.115	
Barnton	523 m (	572 yd)		1777	p.38	
Gannow	511 m (	559 yd)		1801	p.76	
Gosty Hill	509 m (	557 yd)		1797	p.78	
Bruce	459 m (	502 yd)		1810	p.49	*Savernake*
Manchester	456 m (	499 yd)		1839	p.90	Abandoned 1922
Adwick	431 m (	472 yd)		c.1804	p.32	
Chirk	420 m (	459 yd)		1802	p.53	
Aylestone Hill	403 m (	440 yd)		c.1841	p.37	Abandoned c.1881
Shrewley	396 m (	433 yd)		1799	p.107	Features a separate horse tunnel
Saltersford	388 m (.	424 yd)		1777	p.102	
Wellow	370 m (	405 yd)		1799	p.118	Abandoned
Ashperton	365 m (	400 yd)		c.1841	p.35	*Walsopthorne*
Hincaster	347 m (	380 yd)		1819	p.84	Preserved ancient monument
Ashford	343 m (	375 yd)		1799	p.34	
Hardham	343 m (	375 yd)		1790	p.81	Closed 1889
Coseley	329 m (	360 yd)		1837	p.56	Double towpath
Brandwood	321 m (	352 yd)		1796	p.44	*King's Norton* (but see Wast Hill)
Seller's Yard	320 m (	350 yd)		2000	p.105	
Lillesdon	287 m (	314 yd)		c.1839	p.89	Closed 1868
Hyde Bank	282 m (	308 yd)		c.1799	p.86	
Illminster	274 m (	300 yd)		1842	p.86	Closed 1868
Stirchley	257 m (	281 yd)		c.1788	p.111	Destroyed 1860
Yardley	256 m (	280 yd)		1796	p.123	*Stockfield.* Site now covered by a bridge
Snedshill	255 m (	279 yd)		c.1792	p.109	Abandoned 1857
Maida Hill	248 m (	272 yd)		c.1816	p.90	
Whittle Hills	236 m (	259 yd)		c.1804	p.120	Later extended. Abandoned c.1840
Newbold (new)	229 m (	250 yd)		1834	p.93	Double towpath
Snarestone	229 m (	250 yd)		1798	p.108	
Dunhampstead	210 m (	230 yd)		1815	p.65	
Scout	201 m (	220 yd)		c.1799	p.104	Restored 2001
Combe Hay	178 m (	195 yd)		1799	p.55	Closed 1898
Whitehouses	175 m (	191 yd)		1802	p.119	
Woodley	161 m (	176 yd)		c.1799	p.121	*Butterhouse Green*
Drakeholes	141 m (	154 yd)		1776	p.64	
Cwmbran	140 m (	153 yd)		1796	p.62	Restored 1996
Bury	129 m (	141 yd)		1796	p.50	Longer of two tunnels. Abandoned 1961
Newport	128 m (	140 yd)		1796	p.94	Closed 1854
Armitage	119 m (	130 yd)		c.1770	p.33	Opened out
Leek	119 m (	130 yd)		1802	p.89	Restored 1984
Putnal Fields	119 m (	130 yd)		1796	p.99	Abandoned 1858
Newbold (old)	114 m (	125 yd)		1774	p.92	Superseded by new tunnel 1834
Galton	112 m (	122 yd)		1974	p.75	Arched with concrete then buried
Cardiff	105 m (	115 yd)		1794	p.52	*Queen St.* Abandoned 1943
Ashted	103 m (	113 yd)		1793	p.36	
Cricklade	100 m (	109 yd)		1810	p.59	In-filled c.1970
Tuel	98 m (	107 yd)		1996	p.116	Measured round the curve
Edgbaston	96 m (	105 yd)		1795	p.69	
Fallingroyd	94 m (	103 yd)		1986	p.71	Joined prefabricated tube construction
Summit	94 m (	103 yd)		1974	p.114	Arched with concrete then buried
Gibsons	91 m (	100 yd)		1812	p.77	In-filled 1983

Tunnel	Length		Date	Page	Alternative names (*in italics*) & other comments
Rose Hill	91 m (	100 yd)	c.1798	p.100	Opened out
Newnham	86 m (	94 yd)	1794	p.94	Closed 1858
Hag	85 m (	93 yd)	c.1794	p.81	Abandoned 1944
Bates Mill	83 m (	93 yd)	2000	p.39	
Ellesmere	80 m (	87 yd)	1805	p.70	
Cowley	74 m (	81 yd)	1835	p.57	
Deansgate	71 m (	78 yd)	1799	p.63	*Gaythorn, Knott Hill.* Originally longer
Froghall	69 m (	76 yd)	1785	p.74	Very low headroom
Gregory	69 m (	76 yd)	1792	p.79	
Broad Street	69 m (	76 yd)	c.1770	p.48	Much changed since Brindley's original
Brewins	68 m (	75 yd)	1838	p.47	Opened out 1857
Bury	60 m (	66 yd)	1796	p.50	The shorter of two tunnels, closed 1961
Cookley	59 m (	65 yd)	1770	p.55	
Ketley	55 m (	60 yd)	c.1779	p.88	Total of two lengths
Bath No. 1	54 m (	59 yd)	1810	p.40	*Cleveland House*
Curdworth	52 m (	57 yd)	1789	p.61	
Brettell Lane	51 m (	56 yd)	1778	p.46	Opened out 1779
Bath No. 2	50 m (	55 yd)	1810	p.41	*Sydney Gardens*
Buckland Hollow	46 m (	50 yd)	c.1794	p.50	Abandoned 1944
Sowerby Bridge	39 m (	43 yd)	1798	p.111	Closed 1952
Alton	36 m (	40 yd)	c.1809	p.32	Closed [date]
Wolfhampcote	30 m (	33 yd)	c.1774	p.118	Abandoned 1834
Dunsley	23 m (	25 yd)	1770	p.68	*Stourton*
Calne	Length uncertain		c.1809	p.52	Abandoned 1914
Chippenham	Length uncertain		c.1809	p.53	Abandoned c.1900
Oakengates	Length uncertain		c.1792	p.96	Abandoned 1857
Hughes Bridge	Length uncertain		c.1775	p.85	Closed c.1797
Cape Arm	Length uncertain		1772	p.52	Closed to the public

And some anomalies...

Tunnel	Length		Date	Page	Comments
Pensax	3,520 m (3,850 yd)			p.96	Begun 1796, but never completed
Coalport Tar	903 m (	988 yd)	1786	p.54	*Blists Hill.* *Never completed.
Southampton	805 m (	880 yd)	c.1795	p.109	Never properly completed
Ocker Hill	Length uncertain		c.1772	p.96	Small bore - never for navigation
Romford	Length uncertain			p.99	Begun 1875, but never completed

Worsley Mines	*See below			p.122	Begun c.1759-61

*The warren of tunnels comprising Worsley Mines are estimated to total around 74,000 m (81,000 yd). Tunnelling took place continously until around 1889.

The rocky interior of Dunsley

Brick lining inside Sapperton

ADWICK
Dearne & Dove Canal
431 m (472 yds) – Completed c.1804 – Abandoned 1961

The Dearne & Dove canal was approved by Parliament in 1793. William Jessop was too busy to accept the position of chief engineer, with the result that the company first chose John Thompson as their first supervisor. Thompson, however, was soon replaced by that well-known trouble-shooter Robert Whitworth, possibly after the Dearne & Dove began to suffer problems with subsidence. Adwick tunnel was constructed by the 'cut and cover' method. It was apparently unfinished when Whitworth died in 1799, and thus it is believed that the work was completed by one of his sons, William or Robert junior.

Despite its short length, the canal was initially a profitable waterway, although the tunnel stretch was largely bypassed after a deal between the canal company and the North Midland railway in the late 1830s. Eventually the canal came under the control of the Manchester, Sheffield & South Lincolnshire Railway Company, who presided over its gradual decline. The last main customer of the canal - a large colliery - ceased to send coal by this method in 1952. The Dearne & Dove was abandoned in 1961. Since that time, most of the canal, including Adwick tunnel, has been in-filled.

Adwick tunnel lay south-east of Barnsley, near Wath-upon-Dearne in South Yorkshire.

ALTON
Caldon Canal (Uttoxeter extension)
36 m (40 yds) – Completed by John Rennie c.1809
Abandoned 1847

JOHN Rennie and his employers had originally intended to terminate the Caldon canal at Froghall, in 1785, until pressure from the citizens of Uttoxeter forced them to extend the waterway further south. Difficult negotiations with powerful local landowners such as the Earl of Shrewsbury delayed work until 1807.

The eventual line of the extension necessitated a 40-yard tunnel just north of the village of Alton in Staffordshire, together with seventeen locks and an iron aqueduct. Although the completion of the Uttoxeter extension in 1811 was greeted with delirious joy in the town itself, the line was never a success. Within years, competition from the railways meant that the extension was losing £1,000 per year.

When the North Staffordshire Railway Company took over the canal company in 1847, the Uttoxeter extension, together with Alton tunnel, was immediately closed. Large stretches of the canal have now vanished.

Alton tunnel was located just south of the now-famous Alton Towers theme park in Staffordshire.

ARMITAGE

Trent & Mersey Canal
119 m (130 yd) – Completed by James Brindley c.1770
Opened up1971 – fully navigable – towpath

Armitage is thought to have been the first canal tunnel dug in Britain, with the possible exception of those servicing Worsley Mines. As part of James Brindley's project of the Trent & Mersey canal, it dates from around 1770.

Armitage survived as a tunnel for exactly two hundred years, but proved problematic from its earliest days. Local coalmining soon caused distortions in the narrow

The site of the west portal

bore through the unlined sandstone, which in turn caused boats, especially butties, to scrape and bounce off the sides. A combination of continuous subsidence and repeatedly raising the roof to maintain headroom has meant that over two centuries the requirement for a tunnel has been removed.

By the 1970s the giant mine at nearby Rugeley was undergoing closure, a process which included the initiation of a controlled subsidence to allow the land to settle. The thin layer of rock remaining above the tunnel was now removed completely, some of it used to infill the 'cut' where the water had become very deep. The main road that crossed over the old tunnel was rebuilt in the form of a huge concrete plate resting on bearings set well back from the bare rock sides of the canal.

The site of Armitage tunnel remains a peculiar sight on the Trent & Mersey, shady and claustrophobic, and still inhibits the flow of boats along this stretch of the canal.

The tunnel site lies to the west of Armitage on the A513 in Staffordshire.

ASHFORD

Brecon & Abergavenny Canal
343 m (375 yd) – Completed by Thomas Dadford junior in 1799
Just about navigable – no towpath

By convention the Brecon & Abergavenny canal is now a section of the Monmouthshire & Brecon. In 1791 the prospect of the Monmouthshire Canal inspired local leaders such as the Duke of Beaufort to engage Thomas Dadford junior to survey a line to Abergavenny. The project was approved by an Act of 1793.

The south portal

Dadford's younger brother John began to construct a temporary tramroad in 1794, but with Thomas busy with the Monmouthshire project, work on the canal itself was delayed until 1797. Shortage of money proved a frequent obstacle, and the tunnel was not opened until the summer of 1799. The town of Brecon was finally reached in December 1800.

Ashford is the only tunnel on the B & A, and features a masonry lining. The Brecon & Abergavenny prospered for a short time, carrying lime, coal, manure and farm produce, but, like so many other canals, it fell into decline. The canal received no official protection under the 1968 Transport Act, but local councils allied with the BWB and enthusiasts to ensure its survival. This commitment was tested by a collapse in the tunnel in 1984, but happily extensive repairs were effected. A plaque on the south portal commemorates Ashford's re-opening in May 1985.

The tunnel is navigable, although its width of 2.5m (8ft) allows one-way working only. There are gauge bars suspended at both portals to warn of a low point in the middle of the tunnel. Boaters have to duck below the roof level of most modern craft and steer blind for a few metres.

Ashford tunnel lies just south by south-east of Brecon, on the B4558 near Talybont-on-Usk, in Powys.

ASHPERTON

Herefordshire & Gloucestershire Canal
365 m (400 yds) – Built by Stephen Ballard c. 1841
Currently closed but restoration planned - There was a towpath

The Herefordshire & Gloucestershire Canal was built in two distinct stages and took over fifty years to build. The first section from Over (Gloucester) to Ledbury was constructed between 1793 and 1798. The next section, Ledbury to Hereford was begun in 1839 and completed in 1845. Ashperton was built during this second phase.

▲ *Commemorative plaque*

Ashperton was engineered by Stephen Ballard and has a length of approximately 365 metres (400 yards) with a towpath throughout. The tunnel is situated to the west of Ledbury, off the A438 near the village of Ashperton. The tunnel is sometimes recorded as 'Walsopthorne', the name of the manor house close to the west portal.

▲ *The east portal lies below Tunnel House*

The growth of the railways saw the opening of a line from Hereford to Worcester via Ledbury in 1861, which inevitably brought stiff competition and curtailed the economic life of the canal. In 1863 the canal was leased to the Great Western Railway, who intended to convert the Ledbury to Gloucester section into a railway. The eventual building of the line in 1881 severed the Ledbury to Hereford section of the canal from the rest of the country's waterways, and as a result it fell into decline. The canal is slowly being restored by the Herefordshire & Gloucestershire Canal Trust, but this stretch has not yet been acquired. The deep cuttings in which both portals existed have been heavily tipped in over a prolonged period and no brickwork is now visible.

Ashperton tunnel is located just off the A417 in Herefordshire, in a rural area between Ledbury and Hereford.

ASHTED

Birmingham Canal Navigations
103 m (113 yds) – Completed circa 1793
Fully navigable – with towpath

▲ *Inside the tunnel*

Ashted tunnel is of eighteenth century antiquity, and forms part of the Digbeth branch which enables the Birmingham & Fazeley canal to link at Aston Junction with the Grand Union at Bordesley. The link is just under a mile long, rising from Digbeth Basin through five locks to Ashted tunnel. A final lock raises the canal to the level of the main Birmingham & Fazeley at Aston Junction.

This tunnel does not lie at the summit of its hill. As a consequence of this placement it is rare in that the locks leading to one portal (Bordesley) *descend*, whilst those at other portal (Aston) *ascend*.

Ashted also boasts another relatively uncommon feature; internal electric lighting was introduced as part of Birmingham's inner city regeneration scheme. Until five years ago there were rather dangerous gaps in the wooden rail through the tunnel, but these have also happily been rectified.

▲ *The south portal*

Ashted is situated approximately 1/2 mile from Birmingham town centre. The tunnel is passed over by the A47 (Jennens Road). Access is via Aston Science Park, Ashted Circus Roundabout or Belmont Row.

AYLESTONE HILL

Herefordshire & Gloucestershire Canal
403 m (440 yds) – Built by Stephen Ballard c. 1839-1845
Abandoned circa 1881 – Restoration planned – no towpath

The Herefordshire & Gloucestershire Canal was built in two distinct stages and took over fifty years to build. The objective of the company was to link Hereford to the River Severn.

The first section from Over (Gloucester) to Ledbury was constructed between 1793 and 1798. The next section, Ledbury to Hereford was begun in 1839 and completed in 1845. Aylestone and its sister tunnel Ashperton were built during this second phase.

The growth of the railways saw the opening of a line from Hereford to Worcester via Ledbury in 1861, which inevitably brought stiff competition and curtailed the economic life of the canal. In 1863, the canal was leased to the Great Western Railway who intended to convert the Ledbury to Gloucester section into a railway. The eventual building of the line in 1881 severed the Ledbury to Hereford section of the canal from the rest of the country's waterways, and as a result it fell into decline.

The overgrown east portal

The canal is slowly being restored by the Herefordshire & Gloucestershire Canal Trust, but the canal near Aylestone Hill has been filled in for many years. A lot selling second-hand vehicles now stands on top of the in-filled canal next to the western portal of the tunnel.

There is very little water in the tunnel, but the stone work of the eastern portal is in good condition. Light can be seen at the far (western) end. Less than five metres from the entrance, the old canal has been filled in to a level well above the portal. The west portal is inaccessible to the general public.

Aylestone Hill tunnel is located to the north of Hereford city centre, near the A4103. The line of the old canal can hardly be detected - just short ornamental stretches exist. It is possible to access the tunnel at the east portal - but not by boat !

BARNTON

Trent & Mersey Canal
523 m (572 yds) – Completed by Hugh Henshall in 1777
Fully navigable – no towpath

Following the death of James Brindley, it fell to his brother-in-law, Hugh Henshall, to complete the link between the Trent and the Mersey.

Geological problems encountered between Middlewich and Acton necessitated two extra tunnels - Saltersford and Barnton in addition to that already anticipated at Preston Brook.

These three tunnels were at that time the longest and most ambitious attempted. Henshall, under budgetary pressures, succeeded at the cost of sacrificing width and neatness.

The Duke of Bridgewater, finding that the narrow 7' gauge prevented his newly-commissioned 40-ton barges from reaching Middlewich, complained bitterly to Henshall. The Trent & Mersey's chief engineer replied rather lamely that as his Lordship's barges had been constructed after the tunnels had been built, there was no cause for complaint!

The south portal

Barnton has several bulges in its lining, which still obscure the vision of boaters - a problem in a tunnel whose narrowness precludes two-way working. Perhaps with this problem in mind, steam tugs were introduced around 1865, which brought discipline to the water-borne traffic. These vessels incorporated revolving wheels as fenders, as close encounters with the tunnel sides were all too frequent. They lasted until the advent self-powered craft made towing unecessary.

The tunnel lies just south west of the village of Barnton, between Runcorn and Northwich in Cheshire.

BATES MILL

Huddersfield Narrow Canal
83 m (93 yds) – Completed by Costain Ltd in 2000
Awaiting canal re-opening in April 2001– no towpath

The Huddersfield Narrow Canal was officially closed by Act of Parliament in 1944, and many parts of the canal were subsequently purchased by interested parties. One such stretch ran through the centre of Huddersfield, where the canal passed through the Bates Mill complex. As the area was already very built up and space was at a premium, the owners of Bates Mill could only enlarge their premises by filling in the old canal and building on the site. Consequently a four-storey extension was built, obliterating the canal underneath.

This appeared to herald the end of canal life in this area, for in addition to the foundations of the four-storey factory, the old Queen Road South bridge over the canal had formidable steel shuttering on the Bates Mill side. As demolition of Bates Mill was clearly not an option, canal enthusiasts who dreamed of restoring the canal and reconnecting it to the Huddersfield Broad Canal half a mile away faced considerable obstacles.

There was only one solution: in 1999 a contract was awarded to the Costain construction company to make a brand new tunnel under Bates Mill. Because of height restrictions, the path of the tunnel was constructed of steel-reinforced piles set in the floor of the factory. This allowed a top to be laid down across the planned line of the tunnel, thus allowing the factory floor to be rebuilt so that business could resume.

Later all the earth was dug out between the piles without affecting the factory above.

Bates Mill and it sister tunnel half a mile away at Sellars Yard were the last canal tunnels to be constructed in the twentieth century.

▲ *The site of the new tunnel, photographed Oct 1999*

This brand new tunnel is located near to the A616, just to the south of Huddersfield city centre

BATH No.1

Kennet & Avon Canal
54 m (59 yds) – Completed by John Rennie in 1810
Fully navigable – with towpath

The canal age appears to have come relatively late to the prestigious and fashionable spa of Bath. Bath's No. 1 tunnel was completed in 1810. The chief engineer of the Kennet & Avon canal was John Rennie, although John Thomas, as resident engineer would probably have had more day to day involvment with the tunnel.

Bath No. 1 is the longer of the city's two tunnels, which together form an impressive gateway, taking the Kennet & Avon from Sydney Gardens to the picturesque countryside beyond. Cleveland House, the imposing sandstone building above the tunnel, was originally the head office of the Kennet & Avon Canal Company.

The two portals of Bath No. 1 are starkly different in character; that outside Sydney gardens is very plain, whilst the inner portal, by contrast, is quite ornate.

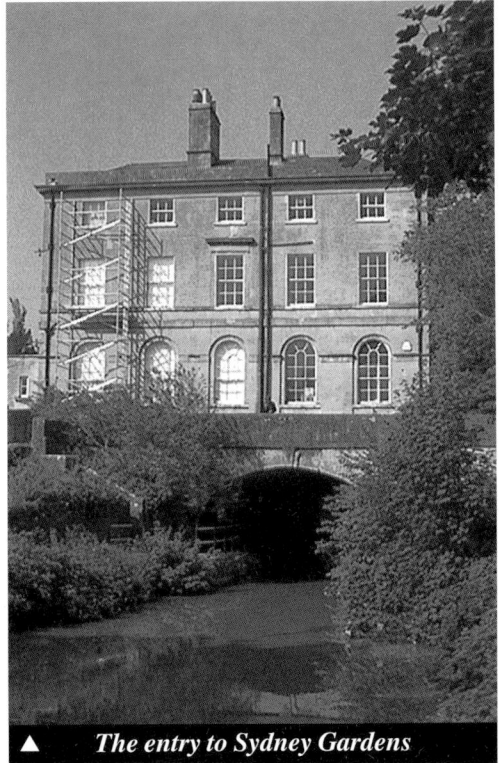

▲ *The entry to Sydney Gardens*

▲ *Detail of the entry portal*

Realising that the inner portals would be seen by genteel visitors to the spa, the canal company no doubt wished to enhance their corporate image! The decorative feature over the inner portal of Bath No. 1 has a female form, whilst that of Bath No. 2 is male.

Inside the tunnel a shaft runs up into the bowels of Cleveland House, and was used to lower messages from the company office to boats on the canal.

Bath No. 1 tunnel can be found at the entrance to Sydney Gardens, on the eastern side of Bath.

BATH No.2

Kennet & Avon Canal
50 m (55 yds) – Completed by John Rennie in 1810
Fully navigable – with towpath

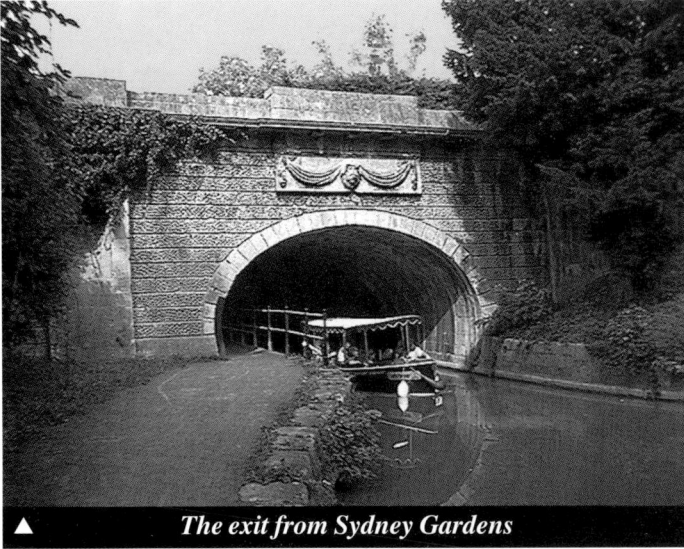

▲ The exit from Sydney Gardens

Bath No. 2 is the shorter of the two tunnels which mark the entrance and exit of the Kennet & Avon canal as it cuts through Sydney Gardens in the east of the city.

Like its sister tunnel the portals of Bath No. 2 are very different from one another. The portal comprising the entrance to Sydney gardens features very little detail or definition in comparison with the ornate inside portal. The main feature of the Bath 2 portal is of a male, whilst that of Bath 1 is of a female.

Efforts to improve navigable access to Bath had begun in the seventeenth-century, and proposals for a canal to the city were submitted as early as 1788. However, costly logistics - and a degree of embezzlement - delayed the commencement of work until the late 1790s. The Bath tunnels themselves, engineered by John Rennie and his resident assistant John Thomas, were opened in 1810.

▲ Detail of the exit portal

Bath No. 2 tunnel can be found by Sydney Gardens on the eastern side of Bath.

BERWICK

Shrewsbury Canal
887 m (970 yds)
Begun by Josiah Clowes, completed by Thomas Telford in 1796
Closed 1839 – wooden towpath until 1819

A huge demand for coal in Shrewsbury led to the proposal of a canal to link the town with nearby Shropshire mines. The scheme was eagerly supported by prominent local businessmen and professionals such as William Reynolds and the Gilbert brothers, as well as landowners such as Lord Gower, a close relation of the 'Canal Duke' of Bridgewater. Parliamentary approval followed in 1793

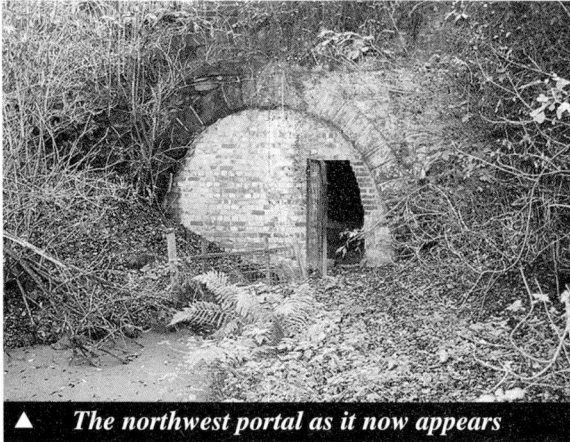

▲ *The northwest portal as it now appears*

Josiah Clowes was employed as chief engineer of the new project, but had died by the time the canal was open to Berwick Wharf (November 1796). It was therefore left to Thomas Telford to complete the canal. Originally known as Preston, the tunnel was planned to be 920 yards in length, but was extended to 970 yards. When officially opened in 1797, it was re-named in honour of Lord Berwick, a prominent landowner and company shareholder.

Berwick was designed without a towpath, but William Reynolds set wood bearers into the wall above the water to support a wooden towpath. This, rather than a standard towpath, allowed water to be displaced more easily by advancing tub-boats, but it fell into desrepair and was removed in 1819.

As the Shrewsbury was designed to accommodate 'tub-boats' from the Shropshire canal, the locks were too narrow for narrowboats. This made the waterway less versatile and vulnerable to competition from the railways fifty years later. When the inclined plane at Trent allowing access to the canal broke down, Berwick tunnel was made redundant. It closed in 1839.

The structure, however, has survived to the present day. Although both portals are bricked up, the tunnel is still in water after over one and a half centuries. Most of the canal network onto which the Shrewsbury had been attached in 1845 was itself closed in 1858.

Berwick tunnel lies two miles east of Shrewsbury and one mile south of Uffingham in Shrophsire, extending from the tiny hamlet of Preston (just south of the A5) to the equally small Berwick Wharf.

42

BLISWORTH

Grand Union Canal
2,794 m (3,056 yds) – Completed by William Jessop in 1805
Fully navigable – no towpath

The south portal

Work on Blisworth began as soon as the Grand Junction canal received Parliamentary approval in 1793. The first attempt failed in 1796 following floods and collapses. The canal's chief engineer William Jessop suggested the building of 29 locks over the hill, but his resident engineer, James Barnes, backed by Robert Whitworth and John Rennie, proposed a new tunnel on a different line. Work restarted in 1802, some two years after the rest of the canal was finished.

In the interim, a toll road had been built over Blisworth hill; but as it could not cope with the sheer volume of traffic a double-track tramroad was laid down by Benjamin Outram. Goods were unloaded from the barges, drawn over the hill by horse and re-loaded on to barges on the other side. When the tunnel finally opened on 25 March 1805 the tramway was largely removed.

Boats were originally poled through, although this was soon replaced by "legging". The registered leggers wore brass company badges on arm bands to advertise their official status. Around 1869 the leggers were replaced by a steam-driven engine which hauled craft through on a continuous wire hauser. This system was replaced by steam tugs in 1871, which themselves survived until 1936. By this time the Grand Junction canal had been incorporated into the Grand Union.

Over the next decades lack of maintenance caused the structure of the tunnel to deteriorate, until it was closed for four years during the 1970s. Following extensive repairs, a revitalised Blisworth was re-opened in 1984. Blisworth is very wet inside. Boats of 7 foot beam can pass in the tunnel, but wider vessels need permission to enter. Unpowered craft and canoes are prohibited.

The tunnel runs from Blisworth to Stoke Bruene, west of the M1 near Northampton and Milton Keynes.

BRANDWOOD

Stratford Canal
321 m (352 yds) – Completed by Samuel Potter in 1796
Fully navigable – no towpath

The traditional trade routes through Stratford-upon-Avon suffered badly after freight began to use the new canal systems linking Birmingham and Bristol. The obvious solution was for the town to have its own waterway links, and the Stratford-upon-Avon Canal Act was duly passed on 28 March 1793.

Surveyors had found few problems in the proposed line from King's Norton to Hockley Heath except for the need for a tunnel at Brandwood. Its close proximity to the Birmingham suburb has actually resulted in some publications referring to Brandwood tunnel as 'Kings Norton', a designation more properly assigned to the tunnel at Wast Hill.

The engineer initially employed on the Stratford canal was Josiah Clowes. Clowes may have begun work on the north end of the tunnel, but died in 1795. It was left to his assistant Samuel Potter to complete the work and open the tunnel on 25 May 1796. Horse-drawn boats had to be hauled through by means of an iron rail along the inside of the tunnel. Parts of this rail are still visible, together with another interesting feature, the profile of a local boy - William Shakespeare - above the east portal.

▲ *Shakespeare's profile over the east portal*

Brandwood tunnel lies in Kings Norton, a suburb of Birmingham.

44

BRAUNSTON

Grand Union Canal
1,867 m (2,042 yds) – Completed by William Jessop in 1796
Fully navigable (permission required for wide craft) – no towpath

Take a short walk down the soggy towpath from the Lord Nelson pub in Little Braunston and you will be rewarded by the pretty little west portal of Braunston tunnel.

The tunnel was an important element in the Grand Junction canal project, which was authorised in 1793. With sponsors such as the Duke of Grafton, the Grand Junction aimed to provide the Midlands waterways network with an all-year-round link to the Thames (the Oxford access to the Thames sometimes dried up). William Jessop was appointed chief engineer, with James Barnes as resident.

At over 2,000 yards, Braunston tunnel was a difficult undertaking, made even more problematical by quicksands and it had been necessary to provide brick lining throughout.

When the tunnel opened in 1796 it presented boatmen with several tricky kinks to navigate .

The tunnel width also caused long queues which led to a ban on wide boats in 1805. Even today, boats over 7' beam require official permission to enter.

Like many canals, the Grand Junction was eventually swallowed up by the Grand Union Canal Company.

▲ *The west portal*

Lack of funds for maintenance caused Braunston to be closed for a considerable period in the mid-1970s, and the severe winter of 1978-9 caused further problems. Happily such issues have now been resolved and the stretch is again one of the busiest in the country.

The tunnel is located in Northamptonshire, between Little Braunston and Welton.

BRETTELL LANE

Stourbridge Canal (later Staffordshire & Worcestershire)
51 m (56 yds) – Completed by Thomas Dadford junior in 1778
Fully navigable – opened out 1779

The intended function of the Stourbridge Canal was to carry coal from the Black Country mines around Dudley to the industrial area of Stourbridge and (via the Staffordshire & Worcestershire canal) to the towns athwart the River Severn. The Birmingham Canal Company opposed the first Parliamentary Bill to establish the Stourbridge, but when proposals were modified, the canal was finally authorised by an Act of 1773.

The scheme had powerful backers, not least local landowning aristocrats Lords Ward, Stamford and Foley. The Foley family in particular had been associated with the ironworking industry around Stourbridge for generations. Thomas Dadford junior was appointed chief engineer, with James Green as his assistant.

At only 56 yards, Brettell Lane was a small tunnel, and it is surprising that a cutting was not attempted from the start.

The delay in unhitching the boat horses to lead them over the top of the tunnel would have been an irritant, added to the fact that mine workings in the local area were notoriously unstable and had affected all tunnels in these parts. Dadford clearly had

▲ *The site of the tunnel, seen from the south*

second thoughts, as the tunnel only existed for one year before it was opened up and a bridge constructed in its place.

Matters had been settled at Brettell Lane before Dadford was replaced by Abraham Lees - who was in his turn suceeded by James Green. The present cutting has a footpath, but the tunnel is not believed to have had one.

The site of Brettell Lane tunnel lies in Brierley Hill, West Midlands. Instead of the tunnel, you will now see a bridge, which carries the A461 from Dudley to Stourbridge.

BREWINS
Dudley No.2 Canal (later BCN)
Length 68 m (75 yds) – Opened (possibly by Thomas Brewin) in 1838
Fully navigable – opened out to a deep cutting 1857

Thomas Brewin was already an influential figure on the committees of several West Midlands canals when the Dudley Canal Company appointed him their superintendent of works in 1812. He became extremely wealthy not only because of a generous salary, but from trading coal wholesale to the Worcester & Birmingham and Stratford canals.

The nineteenth century saw several waves of canal improvement, and Dudley was no exception. A cut-off near Dudley Wood in 1836 discarded 200 yards of canal, whilst a further improved course opened in 1838 saved another 400 yards. This involved a 75-yard tunnel near Lodge Farm, which was named Brewins after the man who had contributed so much to the company both as an official and as a shareholder.

▲ *The site of the tunnel, seen from the east*

Ironically, Brewins tunnel survived scarcely twenty years before it too fell victim to Victorian rationalisation. Between 1857 and 1858, the company instigated a general renovation of the line whilst constructing Netherton tunnel. As part of this programme, Brewins was opened out to the sky.

The deep cutting and bridge where the tunnel once lay can still be seen today. The present cutting features a towpath, and it is fairly certain that the original tunnel also had one.

The site of Brewins tunnel is located approximately two miles south of Dudley in the West Midlands. The main road passes directly over the cutting.

BROAD STREET

Birmingham Canal Navigations
69 m (76 yds) – Designated (or re-designated?) a tunnel c.1976
Fully navigable – double towpath

▲ *The proof!*

Broad Street is one of those tunnels which canal enthusiasts love to argue about. The original "Brindley" canal into Birmingham passed through what is now Cambrian Wharf, to end at Newhall Wharf. The wharf now known as Gas Street basin required the engineers to burrow beneath Broad Street, and hence a tunnel was created here in the late eighteenth century. The original length is unrecorded.

Over the next two centuries, urban development has replaced much of the original tunnel with an artificial superstructure. It now resembles a repeatedly widened bridge, but tradition has dictated that the old "tunnel" nomenclature has been retained.

One building, a church, which stood over on the north side of the old Broad Street tunnel, was demolished in the early 1980s, further erasing clues as to the length of the original structure. All the old warehouses have now been converted to provide leisure venues in this now fashionable quarter.

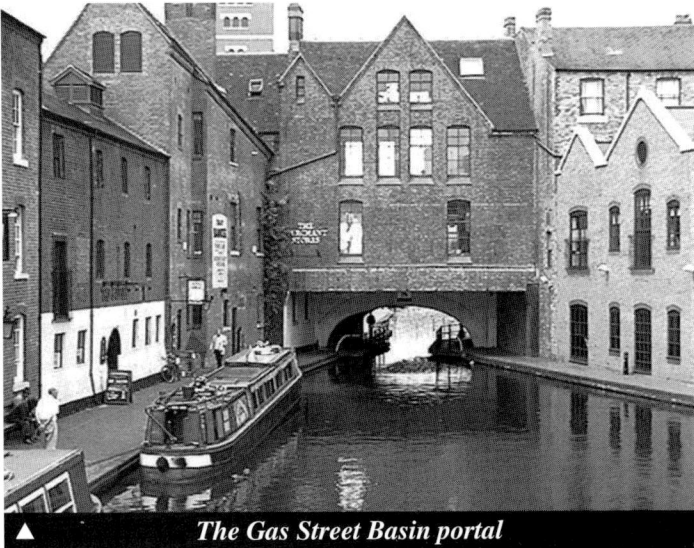

▲ *The Gas Street Basin portal*

Broad Street tunnel is situated under the street of the same name in the heart of Birmingham, next to the International Convention Centre.

BRUCE

Kennet & Avon Canal
459 m (502 yds) – Completed by John Rennie c.1809, opened 1810
Fully navigable – no towpath

The massive east portal of Bruce tunnel may well be one of the largest in the country, indicative of the grandioise ambitions of the canal company and its engineer, John Rennie. Work started on the canal in 1794, but plans were altered almost immediately; changing the route around Crofton in order to shorten the length of the tunnel. Nevertheless, by 1804 Rennie had to admit that he had spent over half a million pounds, and still needed almost £150,000 more to complete.

The east portal

An Act of 1805 allowed the extra funds to be raised, and work recommenced with John Thomas as Rennie's resident engineer. The tunnel at Savernake was completed by 1809, and was diplomatically named "Bruce" tunnel, in honour of Thomas Bruce, Earl of Ailesbury, a powerful local landowner and shareholder.

Despite its huge exterior, Bruce tunnel was constructed without a towpath. Before the days of self-powered craft, boats were pulled through by means of chains embedded along the tunnel walls.

For the next few decades, the Kennet & Avon saw busy commercial traffic between London and Bristol and the shareholders profited enormously. Prosperity came to an abrupt end in 1841, when the Great Western Railway opened a track beside the canal. The drop in income was immediate and cripling. Inevitably, the GWR was soon able to purchase the canal, and supervised its decline. The canal, however, managed to survive several threats of closure, and following an extensive restoration was re-opened by the Queen in August 1990.

Bruce tunnel is located on the edge of Savernake Forest, north of Stibbs Green and just south east of Marlborough in Wiltshire. Because of its proximity to the forest, the tunnel is sometimes known as 'Savernake'.

BUCKLAND HOLLOW

Cromford Canal
46 m (50 yds) – Completed by William Jessop, opened c.1794
Abandoned 1944 – originally featured a towpath

Richard Arkwright was mentor of the Cromford, desiring better communications to his cotton mill at Cromford itself. The leading canal engineer of his age, William Jessop, was engaged as chief engineer, but he found the Cromford a difficult assignment, and battled against inadequate finance, engineering problems and geological obstacles.

When the canal eventually opened in 1794, it enjoyed a brief period of prosperity, carrying coal from the East Midlands. Buckland Hollow, 50 yards long, was the smallest of the Cromford tunnels. In the 1830s competition from the railways (the nearest line built by none other than Josias Jessop - the son of William Jessop) ate into the canal's revenue.

Repeated collapses of Butterley tunnel in the early 1900s cut the canal in half, and it quickly fell into dereliction. Today, whole stretches have disappeared, and two of the tunnels, Hag and Buckland are remembered only in the occasional article.

The site of Buckland Hollow lies among the traces of the Cromford canal between Ambergate and Butterley tunnel, near to the junction of the A610 and the B6013 in Derbyshire.

BURY

Manchester, Bolton & Bury Canal
Two tunnels: 60 + 129 m (66 + 141 yds)
Completed by Matthew Fletcher in 1796
Abandoned 1961

The complicated life of the Manchester, Bury & Bolton Canal began when its construction was authorised by an Act of 1791. The line was surveyed by Matthew Fletcher, later to be appointed chief engineer, and Hugh Henshall, who was retained as a consultant.

The line to Bury was completed in September 1796, with Bolton reached three weeks later. In 1808 a link between Irwell and Bolton completed the canal. Strictly speaking, two tunnels were created at Bury, of 66 and 141 yards respectively.

Unlike many other canal companies, who were hit by railway competition, the forward-thinking board of the Manchester, Bolton & Bury turned themselves into a railway company. The Bury line of the canal survived in isolation until colliery closures in 1951 robbed the waterway of vital income. It was formally abandoned in 1961.

BUTTERLEY

Cromford Canal
2,801 m (3,063 yds) – Completed by William Jessop in 1794
Collapsed 1907 – now derelict – no towpath

With Sir Richard Arkwright as company chairman and William Jessop as Chief Engineer, the auspices for the new Cromford canal were good. Jessop's team also included many able assistants, such as Benjamin Outram and Thomas Dadford senior. From the start, however, there were problems with finance, engineering and geology. Work on Butterley tunnel was delayed when it became necessary to repair the newly-built canal.

The tunnel itself went over budget, but its opening allowed twenty years of success carrying coal from East Midland coalfields. In 1831 serious competition arrived in the shape of a railway, and canal traffic began to decline. The canal tunnel, which was originally 2,966 yards long, had to be lengthened when the railway was built over it. Ironically, the railway engineer responsible was none other than Josias Jessop - the son of William Jessop.

Subsidence at the tunnel site caused a closure in 1889, which, although temporary, effectively killed trade on the canal. In 1900 there was a serious collapse inside the tunnel. This proved to be permanent, for following another collapse in 1907 Butterley never re-opened. A Royal Commission two years later declared repairs to be economically unviable and so matters have remained. To protect the rail line above, the tunnel was reinforced in several places with iron rings made from rail track. Critical points were shored up with hefty timbers, making it impossible to inspect the remaining tunnel properly even by canoe. Despite calls to revive it, the dangerous condition of Butterley tunnel makes re-opening unlikely. The mouth of the tunnel obscured by several decades of silt, and the banks are extremely hazardous. The tunnel today features in many canal books as the quintessential picturesque ruin.

▲ *The overgrown east portal*

The derelict eastern portal lies by the Newlands Inn, on the B6016 just north of Codnor in Nottinghamshire. The western portal lies somewhere on the other side of the A38.

CALNE

Wiltshire & Berkshire Canal
Completed by William Whitworth c.1809 – Abandoned 1914

The Calne Arm of the Wiltshire & Berkshire canal appears to have been constructed under the auspices of the canal's chief engineer, William Whitworth. Whitworth himself was the son of the eminent canal engineer, Robert Whitworth.

The Wiltshire & Berkshire canal was one of a proliferation of waterways in the South West, generating intense competition and ever-lower toll charges which rendered most of them vulnerable to the emerging railways. Most of the Wiltshire & Berkshire had fallen into disuse by 1906, and the canal was formally abandoned in 1914. At present all is quiet around the long-infilled Calne Arm, particularly the stretch leading to the tunnel and the nearby Calne Wharf Lock; however, the Wilts & Berks Canal Amenity Group have an enthusiastic branch in the locality, and hope springs eternal.

The site of Calne tunnel lies under the A4 trunk road near the Wiltshire village of the same name.

CAPE ARM

Birmingham Canal Navigations
Completed by James Brindley in 1772 – Now closed to the public

Cape Arm Tunnel, disused, but still extant, remains one of the shortest tunnels within the historical BCN. The loop was partly filled in to force boatmen to pass the toll office on the new line. Cape Arm is now closed to the public, being located on private property within the GKN complex at Smethwick, Birmingham.

CARDIFF

Glamorganshire Canal
105 m (115 yds)
Completed by Thomas Dadford & son in 1794 – Abandoned 1943

The Glamorganshire canal was designed to link the ironworks and coalmines around Merthyr Tydfill with Cardiff and the coastal trade. Thomas Dadford senior and his eldest son were appointed joint chief engineers with Thomas Sheasby as resident engineer.

The canal was navigable by 1792, but not formally opened until 1794. At one point during the Glamorgan's construction, the canal company actually had their engineers arrested for breach of contract. An inquiry headed by Robert Whitworth exonerated Sheasby and the Dadfords, who were witholding their labour at Cardiff pending arrears of money. By 1885 trade on the canal was in a parlous state. The Glamorganshire closed in 1942, was officially abandoned a year later. There was no towpath, boats being pulled through by chains affixed to the tunnel walls. Whatever remains of the tunnel lies under shops in Cardiff's Queen Street.

CHIPPENHAM
Wiltshire & Berkshire Canal
Completed by William Whitworth c.1809 – Abandoned c.1900

The Chippenham arm of the Wiltshire & Berkshire canal appears to have been constructed under the auspices of the canal's chief engineer, William Whitworth. The Chippenham arm fell into disuse at an early stage in the canal's decline, and was abandoned before the rest of the canal in 1914. The Wilts & Berks Canal Amenity Group have an active local branch, although the long in-filled Chippenham tunnel (located near the intersection of the A420 and the A4 trunk roads in the Wiltshire town) presents a challenge.

CHIRK
Shropshire Union Canal (Llangollen section)
420 m (459 yds) – Width approx. 2.5 m (8ft)
Completed by Thomas Telford & Thomas Denson in 1802
Fully navigable – unlit towpath

The line of the Llangollen (as it is popularly known) was first surveyed by two local contractors, then by William Jessop. The project attracted so much interest that the company was over-subscribed. Jessop was appointed chief engineer, with the two locals, Duncombe and Turner, as his assistants, together with Thomas Denson. A young Thomas Telford was later added to the staff.

Telford's influence and reputation grew, particularly with the bold and successful design of the Chirk aqueduct. When Jessop left in 1801, Telford took over as chief engineer. He and Denson were therefore technically responsible for Chirk tunnel, which was opened in June 1802.

The canal's early success wilted under severe competition from the growing railway network, and it was eventually abandoned in 1944. By 1947, Tom Rolt could not even reach Chirk tunnel due

▲ *The south portal from the aqueduct*

to the collapse of a nearby cutting. Happily, local enthusiasts, supported by Wrexham Rural District Council, saved the waterway from extinction. Matters have improved steadily since the canal was re-classified in 1968.

Chirk tunnel lies on the border between England and Wales, approximately one mile south of the A5.

COALPORT TAR

Shropshire Canal
903 m (988 yds) – Begun by William Reynolds in 1786
Never completed – now dry, but open to visitors

During the eighteenth century, coal was being extracted from the nearby mines in Donnington Wood (now part of Telford, Shropshire), using tunnels dug horizontally from the valley side into the mine workings. Water from the mines was used to flood the tunnel so that tub-boats could float out to a surface canal. Each tub would carry around two tons of coal for use in the region's metalworks.

William Reynolds, planned a similar system at Coalport. A horizontal tunnel was to be driven almost due north into the hillside just above the level of the River Severn with the intention of reaching pitshafts sunk 600 feet from the top of Blists Hill.

The tunnel's construction was not without its surprises; three hundred yards in, the walls began seeping with a thick black liquid (bitumen) - which became worse the further the diggers progressed. Soon, several barrelfuls of bitumen were being removed each day.

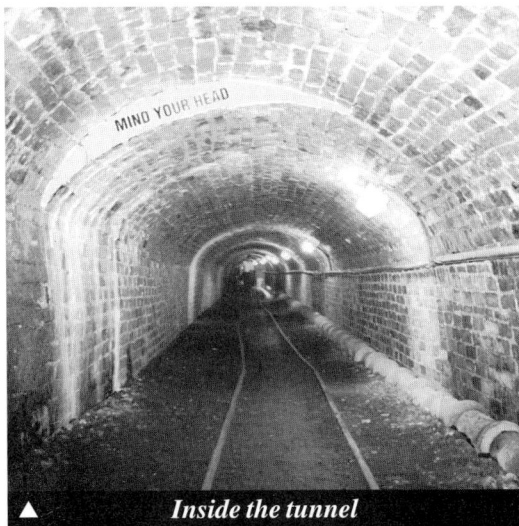

▲ **Inside the tunnel**

In 1787, when the mine shafts were reached, it was decided not to flood the tunnel to create a canal. Instead, it was used as a ventilation shaft and also as a roadway along which wheeled trucks removed the coal. The bitumen proved to be a profitable sideline, with thousands of gallons being sold over the following years.

▲ *A tar pit full of bitumen*

Much of the tunnel is now open as a tourist attraction by the Ironbridge Gorge Museum Trust. After paying an admission charge, it is possible to explore on foot as far as the bitumen accumulations (about 100m from the tunnel mouth). A further length is visible through a grating, and it is planned to open this stretch up as far as a strata of multi-coloured minerals.

Also known as 'Blists Hill' and 'Hay Hill', the tunnel lies by the Severn at Coalport, Shropshire.

COMBE HAY

Somerset Coal Canal
178 m (195 yds)
Completed by William Smith in 1799 – Closed 1898

The Somerset Coal Canal was authorised by an Act of 1794, and opened five years later. William Smith had begun his career as a surveyor, then worked as an assistant engineer on canals further north. Smith appears to have been a competent, but his real fame as the father of British geology lay ahead. He developed his interest in geological strata whilst working on the canal tunnels of the Somerset Coal Canal.

COOKLEY

Staffs & Worcester Canal
59 m (65 yds) – Completed by James Brindley in 1770
Fully navigable – towpath

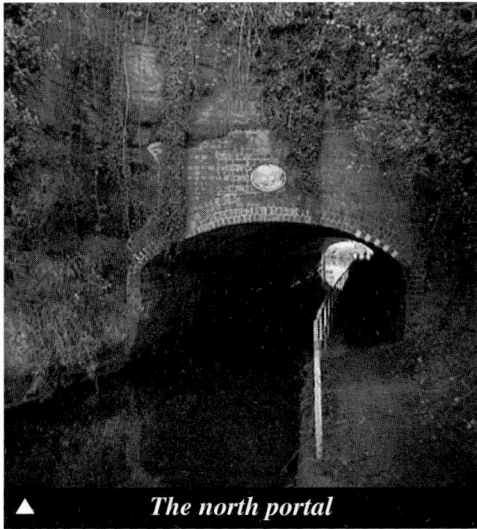

▲ *The north portal*

Cookley is thought to be the oldest navigable tunnel on Britain's canal network - a status made all the more secure by the sad fate of Armitage. Both tunnels, together with Cookley's companion on the Staffordshire & Worcestershire Canal, Dunsley, were overseen by James Brindley. As both were cut, and occasionally blasted, through sandstone rock, it is entirely possible that many of the long-suffering 'navvies' also worked on both.

Brindley, with so many projects underway at the same time, left the actual day-to-day supervision of Cookley to his assistants, Samuel Simcock and Thomas Dadford senior. Theirs was no easy task; the tunnel, which goes under the village of Cookley itself, is three times the length of neighbouring Dunsley. The difficulty of the project perhaps explains the knobbly and untidy appearance of Cookley's insides.

A dearth of traffic in the twentieth century led to moves to close the S&W, but happily the future of the canal, along with its tunnels, was safeguarded by the Transport Act of 1968.

Cookley tunnel runs directly beneath the main road through Cookley, Worcestershire.

COSELEY

Birmingham Canal Navigations
329 m (360 yds) – Width approx. 4.5 m (14 ft)
Completed by Thomas Telford in 1837
Fully navigable – double towpath

Coseley tunnel was conceived as part of Thomas Telford's plan to rationalise the complex and twisted navigation between Birmingham and Wolverhampton. Improvements had become increasingly necessary as commercial carriers and their customers began to despair of the log-jams developing within the Birmingham canal system. Coseley tunnel was the central element of a plan to straighten the line and cut out an obsolete loop near Wolverhampton, thus relieving traffic through the locks at Smethwick.

Plans were drawn up as early as 1818, but the sponsors were clearly unnerved by the magnitude of the task, not least the cost of purchasing land at Coseley together with the coal-mines underneath. Little was done for over a decade - until rumours of a planned railway between Birmingham and Wolverhampton brought matters to a head. The necessary land purchases were made in 1836, and work on the tunnel commenced.

The south portal

Inside the tunnel

Now that matters were urgent, three gangs of labourers worked eight-hour shifts around the clock, but progress was hampered by the hazard of mine-workings. A shaft collapse early in 1837 provided the financiers with a further headache, and took almost eight months to rectify. Despite this, Coseley was open by November that same year, and proved an instant success.

The tunnel passes directly beneath Coseley town centre between Dudley and Wolverhampton.

COWLEY

Shropshire Union Canal
74 m (81 yds) – Begun by William Jessop - in use by 1835
Fully navigable – towpath

The north portal

Cowley was originally designed to be over 630 metres (690 yards) long, but the sandstone rock through which the tunnel was dug easily collapsed.

Cowley is one of the few tunnels which is cut directly out of the rock and is unlined. The entrance into the tunnel has been cut directly through the rock face, and hence there are no stone or brick portals at either end.

The north west entrance is approached through a short cutting and has a large, flat sandstone face. The south east entrance has a long, steep sandstone cutting, indicating the area where the tunnel repeatedly collapsed as it was being dug.

Cowley tunnel can be reached by walking approximately quarter of a mile south from the "Boat Inn" or "Navigation" which border the "Shroppy" in the village of Gnosall, Shropshire.

CRICK

Grand Union Canal (Leicestershire section)
1,397 m (1,528 yds) – Completed by Benjamin Bevan in 1814
Fully navigable – no towpath

Crick was dug as part of a scheme to link the original "Old Grand Union" canal with Oxford in order to gain access to the Thames trade. The engineers had originally planned a 838m (964yd) tunnel, but the discovery of quicksand in 1811 soon caused the project to be aborted. Benjamin Bevan had possibly already noted the present site, which, although offering better ground, required a longer tunnel. Work therefore began on the present tunnel in 1812, and it was completed two years later.

The north portal

Large quantities of treacle were apparently carried on this particular stretch of the canal, which encouraged some villagers to fool gullible visitors with stories of a treacle mine. The tradition is still carried on to the present day at Crick village fete!

A ghost is said to haunt the tunnel at night, although local opinion is divided as to whether the spirit is that of a drowned fisherman or a former lengthman responsible for the tunnel's maintenance.

The route taken by the horses over the tunnel is still traced by the present-day "Boat Horse Lane". Considerable repairs were made to the tunnel in the 1880s, but boaters will today find it in very reasonable condition.

The south portal

The north portal of the tunnel is situated approximately one half mile east of Crick, off the A428. The south portal lies a mile to the south-west.

CRICKLADE

North Wiltshire Canal
100 m (109 yds) – Completed by Robert Whitworth & son in 1810
Infilled c.1970

The North Wiltshire canal joined together the Thames and Severn canal (which ran across its northern end), to the Wiltshire and Berkshire canal (which ran across the southern end). It was just seventeen miles long.

Just south of Latton where the canal joined the Thames & Severn, it passed close to the old Saxon town of Cricklade which was on a small hill with entrenchments. A short, shallow tunnel was constructed, without a towpath, and lined with brick. At first glance this may have seemed extravagant, but a deep cutting would have split farms and required bridges; in addition, the use of locks to raise the pound level up and back down again was impractical due to the lack of a good water supply.

When the railways were built the line crossed the canal above the tunnel, and the owners of the North Wiltshire found it increasingly difficult to compete with the new mode of transport. Eventually canal traffic ceased and the waterway deteriorated. Ironically the remnants of the canal and its tunnel survived the railway.

The tunnel was finally filled with black ash in the 1970's to allow the building of a housing estate east of a lane called "The Fiddle". Only one stone of the north portal now remains visible - adjacent to the old tunnel keeper's house in Bath Road.

▲ *Tunnel house (on right) by the site of the north portal*

North of Swindon, Cricklade tunnel passes under the B4553 westwards out of Cricklade town centre.

59

CRIMSON HILL

Chard Canal
1,646 m (1,800 yds) – Completed by Sydney Hall in 1839
Abandoned 1868 – There was no towpath

For many years prior to 1800 there were wishful schemes to create a canal link across Somerset from the Bristol Channel to the English Channel, which would allow boats to avoid the hazardous waters around Land's End. None came to fruition. When the Bridgwater & Taunton canal opened in 1827, the prospect of this elusive shortcut was one factor in proposing a branch canal to Chard.

The Chard canal was authorised by an Act of 1834. Surveyed by James Green, it was originally intended to be a lockless canal - achieving the assent by means of two lifts and two inclined planes, traversing high ridges by two tunnels.

Appointed engineer in 1835, Sydney Hall made some modifications. Lifts in other parts of England were proving troublesome, so the new design featured four inclined planes and three tunnels plus (to avoid building miles of raised embankment) one lock.

Crimson Hill, the longest tunnel, took nearly four years to complete. It was lined with stone and punctuated by drainage holes. Like the next pound up at Ilminster, Crimson Hill started shortly after an inclined plane.

There was no towpath through Crimson Hill tunnel, and as the canal was primarily designed for tub-boats, most craft could not be legged through. To overcome this problem, chains were installed along the roof to enable boatmen to pull their vessels through.

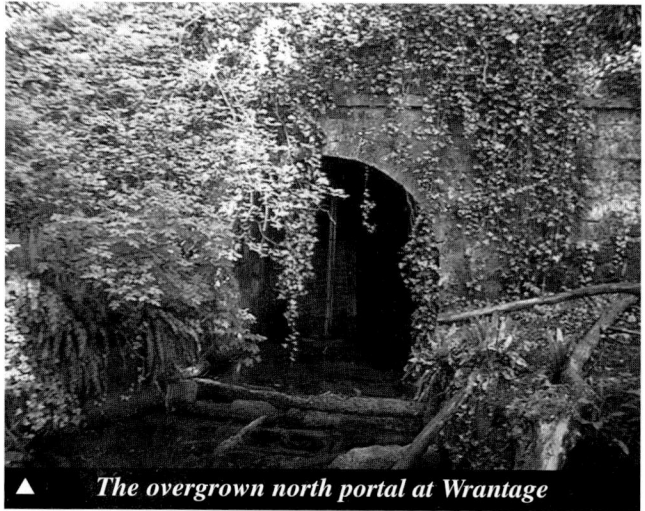

▲ *The overgrown north portal at Wrantage*

The Chard canal proved to be busy, carrying 25,000 tons of cargo per year, but not excessively profitable. It suffered from intense competition when the railway reached Taunton in 1842. The railway to Chard opened in 1866 and the canal closed two years later, after only twenty-six years of use. Despite its ranking among the top twenty canal tunnels in the country, Crimson Hill has almost been forgotten. No discernable traces of the south portal remain, although the north portal has survived.

The site of the south portal lies just to the north of the village of Beer Crocombe in Somerset. The north portal is located close to the Canal Inn, on the A378 near Wrantage.

CURDWORTH

Birmingham & Fazeley Canal
52 m (57 yds) – Completed by John Smeaton in 1789
Fully navigable – with towpath

By the time the Fazeley stretch of the Birmingham and Fazeley canal was finished in August 1789, the company had been swallowed up by their adversary, the Birmingham Canal Company. Eventually the merged company became the famous Birmingham Canal Navigation.

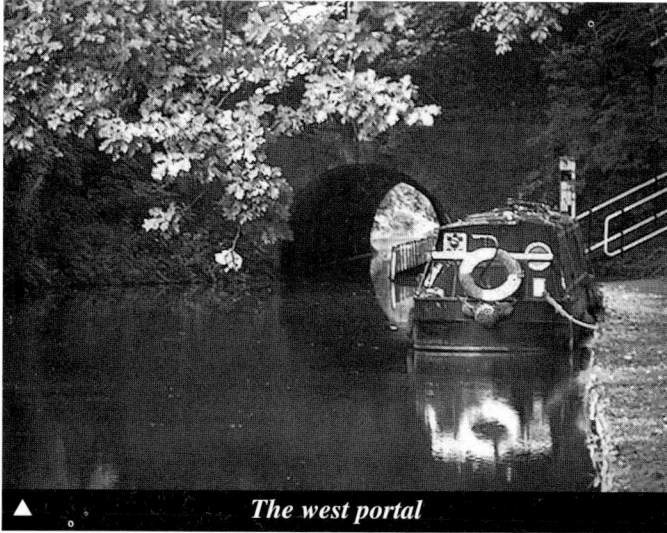

The west portal

John Smeaton, the mentor of William Jessop, was employed as engineer, with John Pinkerton contracted to perform the actual excavations. Although Pinkerton's reputation has been blackened in several canal histories, with stories of drunken incompetence, he appears to have done a reasonable job at Curdworth. The tunnel has, at least, remained in operation to this day.

Unlike many British canal tunnels, Curdworth is currently open to canoes and unpowered craft. Although the tunnel has a towpath, walkers should beware: subsidence of the path at the west end of the tunnel means that the water level of the canal is often the same height as the towpath.

The east portal ▶

Curdworth is just west of Junction 9 of the M42, near Sutton Coldfield in the West Midlands.

CWMBRAN

Monmouthshire & Brecon Canal
140 m (153 yds) – Completed by Thomas Dadford junior in 1796
Navigable with care - no towpath

The Act authorising the Monmouthshire canal was passed in 1792, with the intention of linking inner Wales with the coastal trade, and thus bringing coal and agricultural produce to market more cheaply. In order to open a line between Newport and Pontnewynydd, the canal's chief engineer, Thomas Dadford junior, faced the prospect of a high number of locks; a problem he minimised by constructing two tunnels at Newport, and one at Cwmbran. The line to Pontnewynydd was opened in 1796, with an extension to Crumlin by 1799. The main (Pontnewynydd) line was linked with the Brecon & Abergavenny at Pontymoile in 1812. The boats on this line are said to have been 9'2" in beam - suggesting that Cwmbran tunnel may have required more than usual skill to navigate.

The Monmouthshire Canal Company converted to a railway company in 1845, then acquired the Brecon & Abergavenny. The water network became subservient to the newer mode of travel. Cwmbran gradually lost its significance as stretches of the canal at Newport were filled in. There was no commercial freight to Pontymoile after 1938 and the canal network was progressively closed by Acts of 1954 and 1962.

Happily, the revival of interest in canal travel has reached Cwmbran, and the tunnel stretch was restored in 1996. At the present time, however, navigation ends one mile south of the tunnel. Cwmbran currently has low headroom and very shallow water, hence boaters may hear their vessel scraping along the shale on the canal bed!

The south portal

Cwmbran tunnel lies approximately five miles south of Pontypool in south Wales.

DEANSGATE

Rochdale Canal
71 m (78 yds) – Original completed by William Jessop c.1799
Fully navigable – with towpath

After several attempts, thwarted by various vested interests, the Rochdale canal was finally authorised in 1794. William Jessop was appointed chief engineer, with William Crossley as resident. The northern section of canal from the junction with the Calder & Hebble was opened in 1798; whilst the section through Manchester, including Deansgate tunnel, was probably finished in 1799. The complete navigation was opened in 1804.

▲ *The east portal*

The canal was at first extremely busy and enjoyed a substantial income, carrying coal, stone, corn and lime. Carrying companies such as Pickfords ran regular services from Manchester to Todmorden. Like so many other canals, the Rochdale suffered severe competition from the railways, but commercial traffic survived as far as Sowerby until 1939. By 1948 the Rochdale was derelict in many places. Ironically, the loss of the Anderton lift in the 1980s led to a new lease of life for Deansgate tunnel. A consortium led by the BWB and local Manchester authorities revived a stretch of the canal through the city in order to ensure the integrity of the important Cheshire ring.

Sowerby and Deans gate were originally the only tunnels on the Rochdale, until Fallingroyd and Tuel were constructed in modern times. Deansgate tunnel is also known by the names "Gaythorn" and "Knott Mill". Jessop's tunnel was originally 376 yards long (according to Paget-Tomlinson) or 336 yards long (according to Gagg), but successive waves of industrial development have reduced the tunnel to its present length. It is now effectively a girder bridge. There is today a towpath through this tunnel, although it may not initially have featured one.

▲ *Inside the tunnel*

The tunnel is located under Deansgate in the centre of Manchester

DRAKEHOLES

Chesterfield Canal
141 m (154 yds) – Completed by Hugh Henshall in 1776
Fully navigable - no towpath

The initial survey of the Chesterfield canal was undertaken by John Varley, a protege of James Brindley. After Brindley's death, his brother-in-law Hugh Henshall took over as chief engineer. Despite some criticism of his family's work, Varley remained as resident. The West Stockwith end of the canal was the last stretch to be completed, with Drakeholes tunnel opened to commercial traffic in August 1776.

Whereas the collapse of Norwood tunnel further down the canal killed movement on that stretch of the Chesterfield, the West Stockwith to Worksop line continued to carry coal and products for the metal industry. A further unexpected boost came during World War Two when HM Government, with many airfields in the vicinity, needed to transport tons of munitions.

The south portal

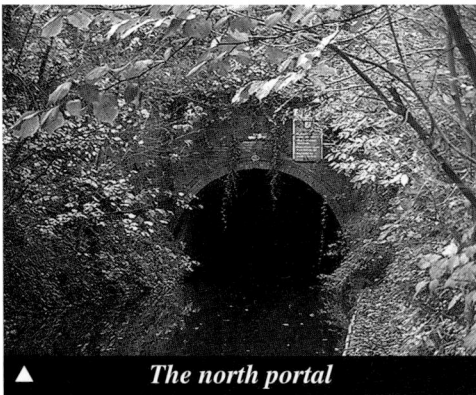

The north portal

By the late 1950s, the line was again under threat. Enthusiasts held rallies to mobilise support for its retention.

Proposals in the 1960s were rather kinder to the West Stockwith-Worksop line than to the rest of the Chesterfield canal below Norwood, suggesting the former could function as a pleasure cruise-way, while the latter become merely a source of water. Drakeholes tunnel has consequently remained in constant use since its inception.

The tunnel lies four miles west of Gainsborough, stradling the B6045 by the White Swan Hotel.

DUNHAMPSTEAD

Worcester & Birmingham Canal
210 m (230 yds) – Completed by John Woodhouse in 1815
Fully navigable – no towpath

Dunhampstead was the last of the five tunnels on the Worcester & Birmingham canal to be opened. Completion was some eighteen years after the Wast Hill tunnel at Kings Norton. It is uncertain how much of this delay was due to the lack of funds experienced by the Worcester & Birmingham Canal Company around 1807.

The south portal

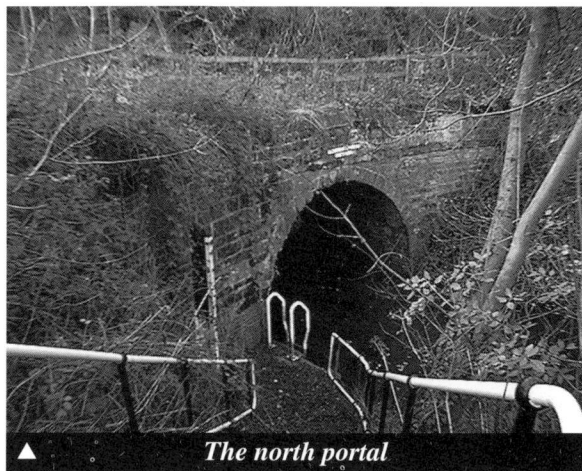

The north portal

Dunhampstead is relatively inconspicuous when compared with the other tunnels on the Worcester & Birmingham Canal. Dunhamptstead, in common with Wast Hill, Shortwood and Tardebigge, did not have a towpath. Unlike its sister tunnels, Dunhampstead did not have the services of a tug to pull boats through. Consequently craft had to be legged from one end to the other.

Regular commercial traffic ceased in the early 1960's, but the Worcester & Birmingham remains a popular canal with pleasure cruisers.

The tunnel is situated to the south east of Droitwich, Worcestershire, south of the B4090. Access is via a walk along the towpath from either bridge 30 or 31.

DUDLEY

Dudley No. 1 Canal (later BCN)
Nominally 2,884 m (3,154 yds), but the subject of heated debate!
Main section opened 1792, but new cross-links have been added
Navigable (with restrictions) – no continuous towpath

In 1775, the 2nd Viscount Dudley and Ward, an important local landowner, began a branch canal linking the Birmingham Main Line to his limestone workings at Castle Hill. The last 226 yards of the 755-yard canal tunnelled in the direction of Dudley Castle (now famous for its zoo) in order to reach the quarry. The new waterway, known as Lord Ward's canal, was completed by 1778. At the same time, Lord Ward had promoted the building of a separate canal south of Dudley to join the existing Staffordshire & Worcestershire line.

Completed in 1779, this gave access to the River Severn and coastal waters via the Bristol Channel.

It was easy to imagine a network of canals radiating from Dudley to all four corners of Britain - if only the Birmingham navigations could be joined to those in Worcestershire. The two networks were less than two miles apart but separated by a formidable obstacle - a high ridge that could not be bypassed. At this time, the Severn and the Thames were being linked by a canal which, in order to traverse the Cotswolds, had to pass through a long tunnel; Sapperton, near Cirencester. Engineers began to consider whether it would be possible to dig a tunnel from the Castle Hill quarries to Park Head, south of Dudley. Following surveys which confirmed that the extension was feasible, a Bill was passed through Parliament on 4 July 1785.

The proposal set out in the Act called for one and three-quarter miles of tunnel, 14 ft high and 9 ft wide, holding a 5 ft depth of water. John Snape and Abraham Lees mapped out the line and the shafts to be dug at intervals along its course. John Pinkerton was given the contract for actual construction.

By October 1785 excavation had begun at Park Head, supervised by Lees and Thomas Dadford senior, the consultant engineer. However, the next three years saw a catalogue of misfortune: Dadford resigned, Pinkerton and the company building the locks were dismissed; Lord Ward died and, with monies low, work came to a grinding halt. Two local engineers, Isaac Pratt

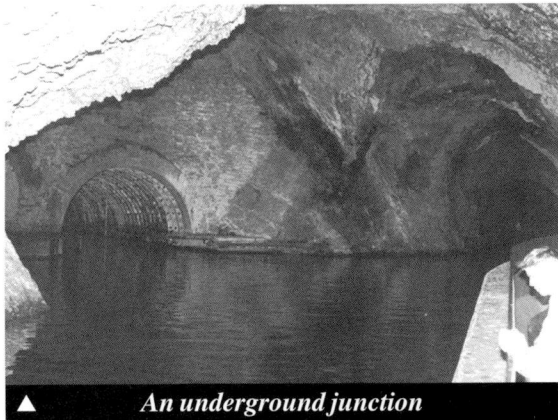

An underground junction

and Richard Aston, tried their best but lacked the expertise to revive the project.

At this point, Josiah Clowes entered Dudley's story: Fresh from completing the two-mile Sapperton tunnel, Clowes made rapid progress; in 1790 the final shaft at Caddick's End was sunk and Castle Mill Basin opened up, providing ventilation, loading bays and passing space. By 1792 the constituent parts of the tunnel had been joined together. Shafts not required for ventilation were then filled or capped and stop locks were installed. That autumn the tunnel was complete - but four years behind schedule. In the meantime competitors, the Oxford & Coventry canal and the Grand Junction had already provided a link from London to Merseyside.

Despite its early problems Dudley tunnel proved a great success, soon exceeding 40,000 boat passages per annum. The railways could not compete with the Black Country canals for short haul bulk shipment, and between 1792 and 1815, many more extensions and improvements were made. One branch tunnel alone (the link to the lime workings at Wren's Nest) added 1,185 yards to the length of the network.

In 1846 the Dudley canals amalgamated with the BCN, forming a stronger, more ambitious company. In 1858 the parallel Netherton tunnel opened as a more modern successor to traffic-choked Dudley. In contrast to Netherton's two-way traffic, double towpath and gas lighting, Dudley tunnel began to show its age; in 1884, 191 metres near the south end had to be rebuilt to a larger bore following subsidence. Traffic volume diminished progressively after 1858, until the tunnel was finally closed and sealed in 1962.

In 1964 a society formed to restore both canal line and tunnel. With a grant from Dudley Council and assistance from British Waterways the tunnel re-opened in 1973. From 1979 the Black Country Museum provided many customers for boat trips. In 1981, a major collapse in the southern section closed the tunnel for ten years. This has now been rectified. Two new link tunnels, bored in the 1980s, allow Dudley Canal Trust to run underground circuit trips.

▲ *The Tipton portal*

The north portal (Tipton) is located within the Black Country Living Museum on the A4037 Tipton Road in the West Midlands. The south portal (Park Head) lies in a public open area off Holly Hall Road, Dudley. The tunnels are navigable to low-top boats that pass the gauge test at either portal. Boats must be towed through by electric tug. Dudley Canal Trust makes no charge for this service, although voluntary donations are always welcome.

DUNSLEY

Staffs & Worcester Canal
23 m (25 yds) – Completed by James Brindley & assistants in 1770
Fully navigable – with towpath

Dunsley, sometimes known as Stourton Tunnel, is something of a minnow amongst canal tunnels, being one of the smallest in the country. It is, however, one of the oldest surviving tunnels still open to navigation.

The south portal

After an initial survey by Hugh Henshall, James Brindley was engaged as chief engineer. Brindley, with work to distract him elsewhere, left the actual supervision of the canal and tunnel to his assistants Samuel Simcock and Thomas Dadford senior. Dunsley was built to Brindley's favoured 7' gauge, and opened in 1770.

The only real threat to the continued existence of Dunsley came in 1959, when the British Transport Commission recommended that the Staffordshire and Worcestershire close and its old rival the Worcester & Birmingham canal be retained. Protesters immediately formed the Staffordshire & Worcestershire Canal Society. With their IWA allies, these enthusiasts managed to fend off extinction until the Transport Act of 1968 guaranteed the canal's survival. Today, maintained by the BWB, Dunsley tunnel remains healthily busy. The tunnel has been cut directly through the sandstone outcrop. It is unlined, except for a short part of the northern end where lining has been added to stop the rock crumbling.

The tunnel lies close near to Stewponey Lock, which is situated at the junction of the A449 and A458, opposite the "Stewponey" pub, approximately five miles north of Kidderminster, Worcestershire.

EARDINGTON

Eardington Forge Canal
549 m (600 yd) – Completed in 1792 – Closed 1889

The Eardington Forge canal was constructed in 1792, and was designed to join the upper forges at Eardington, Shropshire, with those lower down. The tunnel itself was 9 feet wide, but only 6 feet high. It was dug through a hill where the canal ran by the River Severn, three miles south of Bridgenorth. The closure of the forges and a cessation of movement in pig iron robbed the canal of its raison d'etre. The waterway closed in 1889.

The tunnel was situated just south of Bridgnorth, in Shropshire

EDGBASTON

Worcester & Birmingham Canal
96 m (105 yds) – Completed by Thomas Cartwright in 1795
Fully navigable – with towpath

The Worcester & Birmingham canal, authorised by an Act of 1791, effectively gave the manufacturers of the West Midlands an all-season waterway via Worcester to the port of Bristol. It also posed a serious threat to the local monopoly of the Birmingham Canal Navigations, who obstructed the new venture at every turn.

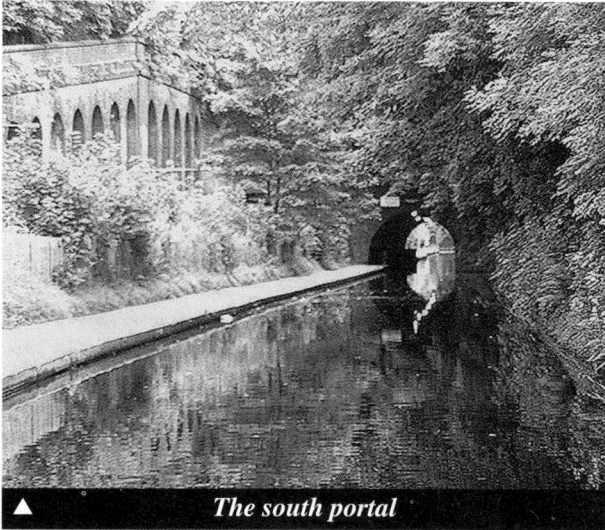

The south portal

Thomas Cartwright, who was to be chief engineer of the Worcester & Birmingham until 1809, began work on the canal at the northern end. On 30 October 1795 the stretch between Birmingham and Selly Oak was opened. This stretch included a tunnel at Edgbaston, approximately two miles from Birmingham city centre. At 105 yards, Edgbaston is the shortest of the five tunnels on the canal, and it is still the only one that can boast a towpath.

The Worcester & Birmingham proved highly successful, although the coming of the railways hit trade hard. The railway line that runs next to the tunnel dates from 1841. In later years the Worcester & Birmingham benefited from the support of George Cadbury, and continued to carry chocolate crumb to Bournville until 1961. Coal trade had ceased the year before and the canal had to survive several closure scares until its future was secured. It now enjoys a degree of security, having become one of the most important cruiseways in the country.

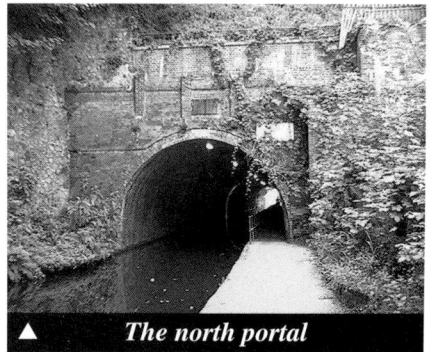

The north portal

The tunnel is accessible from The Vale, Birmingham. The public access point is beside bridge 84A leading to Birmingham University halls of residence (private property).

69

ELLESMERE

Llangollen Canal

80 m (87 yds) – Completed by William Jessop & Thomas Telford in 1805
Fully navigable – towpath (with puddles!)

Plans were made to link the River Mersey to the River Severn from 1790 onwards. Three routes were proposed for the "Ellesmere canal", but in the end none of them were completed. A canal was constructed through Ellesmere which linked Chirk to Grindley Brook near Whitchurch, although it never reached the intended terminus of Shrewsbury. This canal has come to be known as the Llangollen (the actual terminus); but interestingly, not only was it initially called the Ellesmere (because the town occupied a central position on the line), but Netherpool on the Mersey was actually re-named "Ellesmere Port" to promote the enterprise.

Ellesmere was intended to be the hub of many canal branches spreading in all directions, and major workshops and wharves were built there in anticipation. In the end, plans changed and the Shropshire Union canal was built to link Merseyside to the Midlands, and the Severn at Stourport.

The north portal

The tunnel at Ellesmere, with its cuttings on either side, avoided the need for lockage over its wooded hill. As Llangollen is the highest point, the canal is now used for the transfer of around 2,000,000 gallons of water per day from the Welsh hills to reservoirs at Nantwich which then supply the surrounding Cheshire towns.

The Llangollen canal, used mainly for agricultural traffic in the past, is today one of the most popular holiday routes in Britain.

The tunnel lies just to the east of the small Shropshire town of Ellesmere, which is situated between Shrewsbury and Oswestry, close to the Welsh border.

FALLINGROYD

Rochdale Canal
94 m (103 yds) – Completed by West Yorkshire C.C. in 1986
Fully navigable (low headroom) – No towpath

In 1939, the Rochdale canal closed, having suffered a continuous decline in commercial useage caused mainly by competition from the railways which had arrived in the mid nineteenth-century. In the 1970's the original masonry arch between Hebden Bridge and Mytholmroyd was demolished to improve the alignment of the A646. The disused canal beneath was reduced to a three foot diameter culvert, as this stretch of the Rochdale canal was still used to supply water to industry.

As proposals to restore the canal gathered pace, it became clear that a new tunnel would be required under the trunk road in order to make the stretch navigable again. Fallingroyd thus came into being, a curved tunnel constructed from four prefabricated tubes joined at angles. The opening ceremony, held on 21st November 1986, was very reminescent of those held in the previous century; the Mayor of Calderdale and other dignitaries rode aboard the *Sarah Siddons*, which was towed through the tunnel at the head of a flotilla of ten boats.

▲ **The east portal**

A horse-drawn trip from Hebden Bridge marina regularly includes a session of 'legging' through the tunnel. Lying on top of the boat, the pilot is able to reach the tunnel roof with his legs and push the boat through in traditional style.

The tunnel is made up of four straight tubes of reinforced concrete, joined at a slight angle to each other to produce a progressive curve effect. The inner surface is corrugated so boats have to be careful not to jam any protusions into the grooves. The cross section of the profile shows that the bottom is flatter than the curved 'walls' visible above the water rising to the apex. This ensures that when boats pass in opposite directions, they do not hit a 'shallow' near the sides.

▲ **The west portal**

Fallingroyd tunnel passes under the A646 Burnley Road between Hebden Bridge and Sowerby Bridge in the Pennines, on the border between Lancashire and Yorkshire.

FENNY COMPTON

Oxford Canal

307 + 413 m (336 + 452 yds) – Completed by Samuel Simcock in 1778
Opened out 1868-1870 – The present site has a towpath

When the Oxford Canal was first built, Fenny Compton was conceived as a single narrow-gauge tunnel, 1,040 m (1,138 yds) long. Brindley made the original surveys, but after his death it was left to the great man's asssistant Samuel Simcock to see the project to completion. Simcock began work on the tunnel in May 1776, which proved difficult to dig, and ended up only 2.8 m (9 ft 4 ins) wide and 3.6 m (12 ft) high.

This restricted width meant single line working, which in turn caused considerable problems with canal traffic. The problem was partly resolved in 1840 when the land above the tunnel was purchased. A central passing place of 142m (155 yds) was opened up with a tunnel on either side. However, this solution did not entirely resolve the

The site formerly covered by the tunnels

problem, and both tunnels were eventually opened out after the land above was acquired. The work of opening the southern tunnel was completed in June 1868, with the northernmost tunnel being opened out in August 1870.

All that remains today to indicate that any tunnel existed on this site is the aptly named Tunnel Bridge (No. 137) at the north end of the cutting - and the sudden long, straight narrow section of canal as it pushes southwards. Although the sides of the cutting are reasonably high, they have been cut back and disguise the previous existence of two tunnels.

The Fenny Compton tunnels in Warwickshire have been opened out and are no more. The cutting which once contained the tunnels is accessed by using the towpath from either the Wharf Inn, at Fenny Compton Marina at the north end, or half way down via a path leading from the A423.

FOULRIDGE

Leeds & Liverpool Canal
1,500 m (1,640 yds) – Completed by Robert Whitworth in 1796
Fully navigable (low headroom) – no towpath

Pending the re-opening of Standedge tunnel in 2001, Foulridge lies on the only navigable cross-Penine link by canal.

Foulridge tunnel took five years to build, mainly because the labourers were forced to tunnel through loose rock. Due to this problematical geology, the tunnel was constructed in several phases; first, the line was cut out from above. Next, the engineers built an arch, and finally covered the structure with the original spoil. The tunnel finally opened on 1 May 1796.

The tunnel suffered from collapses, and would

The Barrowfield portal

often close in dry summers due to low water levels. A partial collapse in 1824 closed the tunnel for eighteen months. Subsidence remains a problem, amply demonstrated by the gauges at both portals. Interestingly, in view of its original method of construction, there was once a proposal to open the tunnel out.

Foulridge has many tales to tell, both comic and tragic: In 1882, legging was stopped and steam tugs introduced, after a legger suffocated in the tunnel. Most famously of all, in 1912 a cow called Buttercup fell in the canal at the west portal and swam the length of the tunnel. The exhausted animal was apparently revived by medicinal brandy!

The Barrowfield portal features an interesting collection of masons' marks, as does Foulridge's sister tunnel Gannow some miles to the south. The date of 1792 over the portal is curious, as work was not completed by this date. Although Foulridge is quite wide, the low headroom precludes two-way working, and has necessitated the installation of traffic lights.

The east portal

The eastern portal lies near to Foulridge Wharf, which itself is signposted from the A56 running through Foulridge, Lancashire. The western, or Barrowfield portal, lies just west of Foulridge.

FROGHALL

Caldon Canal
69 m (76 yds) – Completed by Hugh Henshall in 1785
Fully navigable (very low headroom) – no towpath

The idea of a canal between Wedgwood's Etruria works and Leek had stalled when James Brindley caught a chill and died whilst surveying the line. In 1775, Wedgwood commissioned a new survey from Hugh Henshall. The Trent & Mersey company liked the idea of an extra water supply for their main-summit, and the trade that would come from access to Lord Shrewsbury's limestone quarries around Cheadleton.

The east portal

Froghall tunnel itself was required, ironically, because of the inefficiency of an existing horse-drawn railroad. The local colliery owners contributed £5,000 to the tunnel project and work began in 1784. The tunnel was open by March 1785.

Froghall participated in Caldon's century of success, but by 1948 the golden days were a distant memory, and links to Froghall and Leek were officially declared un-navigable. The continuing usefulness of the Caldon as a water supply, however, saved the canal from extinction. Fired by the threat of complete closure, local authorities and canal enthusiasts banded together in 1963 to revive the Caldon and its tunnels. Froghall received much-needed repairs to its brickwork in 1972, during an intense two-year programme of restoration of the canal.

In 1983 the Caldon was upgraded to the status of cruiseway. Froghall tunnel is a popular terminus and its immediate future secure - even if unwary pleasure boaters encountering the low headroom regularly add new scars to its battered brick lining!

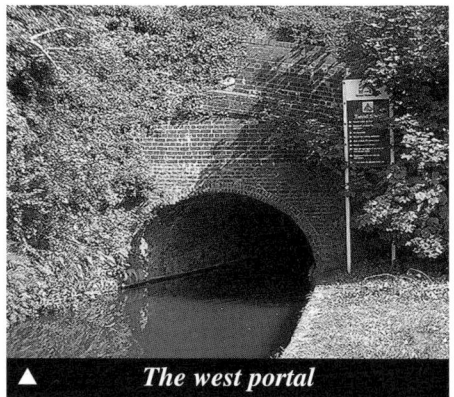

The west portal

Froghall is located just off the B5053 where it meets the A52 in Froghall, Staffordshire.

74

GALTON

Birmingham Canal Navigations
112 m (122 yds) – Completed by the Dept. of Transport in 1974
Fully navigable – with towpath

Galton Valley contains the two Birmingham canals engineered by Thomas Telford and James Brindley. Telford's canal was built to shorten the route between Birmingham and the Black Country and overcome the continual criticisms of Brindley's old looping route.

The deep cut, which is Galton Valley, was crossed by means of a high, elegant bridge made of cast iron inspired by the Darby-made structure at Ironbridge. In the 1970's the Galton bridge became a listed monument, and is now used solely as a footbridge. Traffic was re-routed along a modern dual carriageway, spanning both canals.

▲ *Galton bridge & west portal*

Instead of building an expensive high-arch or suspension bridge, the decision was taken to fill the valley, and build the road on top. To facilitate this, each canal was covered with long prefabricated concrete tubes, which were then earth-filled over the top. These structures are now known as Galton and Summit tunnels.

Galton and Summit afford the highest headrooms of any tunnels in the UK. They boast generous towpaths and sufficient width for boats to pass inside. The project was completed in 1974.

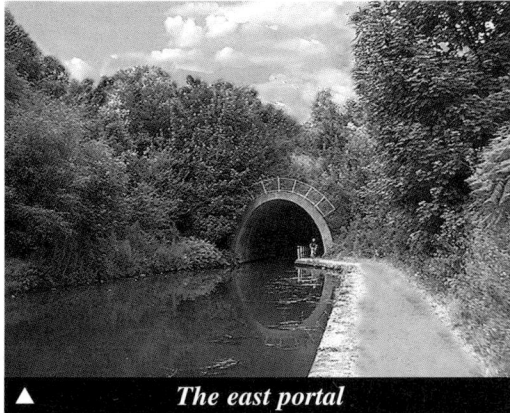

▲ *The east portal*

The tunnel was made much longer than the width of the road above to allow the earth fill to consolidate without side restraints - hence the concrete 'tube' extends beyond the bank above. No attempt was made to construct portals. Trees and shrubs have completely covered the road banks, and the busy trunk road joining Smethwick to the M5 has been masked from the view of canal users.

Galton, on the Birmingham Main Line canal, and its sister tunnel, Summit on the adjacent Brindley line, are located between Birmingham and West Bromwich, just east of the M5 motorway.

GANNOW

Leeds & Liverpool Canal
511 m (559 yds) – Completed by Robert Whitworth in 1801
Fully navigable – no towpath

The Leeds & Liverpool, long desired by business men in the region, took 46 years to come to fruition. The initial burst of canal building, supervised by John Longbotham, came to an end with the recession caused by the American War of Independence. It was not until 1790, with the appointment of Robert Whitworth, that the route through East Lancashire was revived. The line through Burnley, including Gannow tunnel, opened in 1801.

▲ *The north portal*

The tunnel is often overshadowed by two spectacular canal features nearby; the aqueduct over the M65 is impressive enough, but the huge embankment was chosen by John Gagg as "one of the Seven Wonders of the Waterways". Ironically, it was constructed using the spoil from Gannow tunnel and its cuttings.

Like Foulridge on the same canal, the south portal of Gannow is covered in masons' marks; if anything these are more prominent and numerous than the sister tunnel. Until Standedge is re-opened on the Huddersfield Narrow Canal, the tunnels of the Leeds & Liverpool allow access to the only navigable canal across the Pennines.

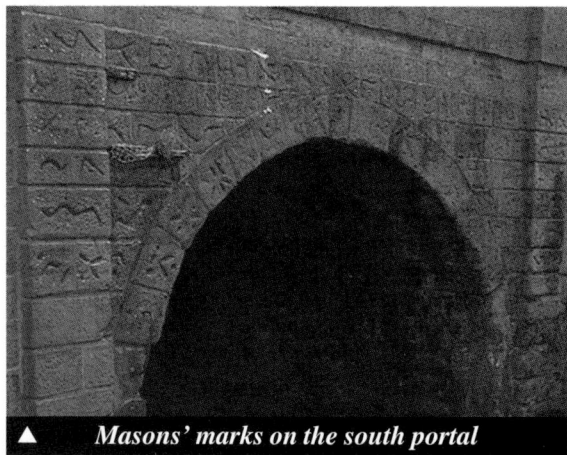

▲ *Masons' marks on the south portal*

Gannow appears to have enjoyed a quiet, relatively trouble-free existence, which is a testament to the skill of Whitworth and his craftsmen, whose masonic marks can still be seen on the south portal.

Gannow nestles around Junction 10 of the M65, where it passes close to Burnley in Lancashire.

GIBSONS

Birmingham Canal Navigations
Probably under 91 m (100 yds) – Completed 1812
Obliterated 1983

Gibson's Arm was built in 1812 to allow narrowboats to pass under The Crescent into Gibsons and Baskerville basins off Broad Street. As the locality was full of warehouses and factories honeycombed with narrow cobblestone passages for horses and carts, canals were the main thoroughfares. The Baskerville factories housed huge printing presses and much industrial innovation occurred there.

▲ *The site of the south portal*

The basins were slightly higher than the 473 ft (Brindley) level, so boats entering via the tunnel had to enter a lock to raise them up. The canal at Crescent Wharf became known as the Newhall Branch even though it was actually the main canal line built by James Brindley in 1769 and extended in 1772. Farmers Bridge locks, still in use today, were not built until 1789.

Gibsons ceased to be used around 1920. The lock was filled in in 1936 to facilitate the foundations of Baskerville House, a prestigious civic building.

The tunnel itself was filled in 1983 when a multi-storey car park was built at Cambridge Street. Part of the old tunnel now lies buried beneath a 'city centre garden' at the rear of Birmingham Repertory Theatre.

In 1812, heavy cargo carrying took place 24 hours a day. Today, only pleasure craft use the nearby navigations - and all movement is restricted to the hours of daylight.

▲ *Cambrian Wharf looking towards tunnel site*

Gibsons was originally located in the centre of Birmingham (on a branch canal off Cambrian Wharf) near to the present site of the International Convention Centre. The tunnel site now lies under the City Centre Gardens, at the rear of the Birmingham Repertory Theatre.

GOSTY HILL

Dudley No. 2 Canal (now BCN)
509 m (557 yds) – Completed by Benjamin Timmins in 1797
Fully navigable – no towpath

The completion of the first Dudley canal after sixteen years of frustration appeared to give the long-suffering sponsors new appetite; Dudley No. 2 canal was proposed at a meeting in August 1792 with an Act a year later. The line surveyed by John Snape initally called for three tunnels, but in the event only two were needed: Lapal and Gosty Hill.

Josiah Clowes, the hero of Dudley tunnel, was chosen as chief engineer with William Underhill as his resident.

The north portal

The huge tunnel vent

Underhill struggled so much after Clowes' death in 1795 that his employers brought in Robert Whitworth to advise. On Whitworth's recommendation, Underhill was given responsibility for the works nearest the junction with the old line. Benjamin Timmins, appointed to oversee the remainder of the canal, took charge of excavations at Gosty Hill, and brought it to completion in 1797.

Gosty Hill, originally designed to be 648 yards, does not appear to have presented such problems as its giant neighbour, Lapal, but it was far from flawless. In 1881 Victorian engineers found it necessary to rebuild almost the whole tunnel.

When Lapal staged its final collapse in 1917, Gosty Hill became essentially the end of the Dudley No. 2 navigation. Today the tunnel's main claim to fame is its enormous vent.

Between the long tunnels of Netherton and Lapal, the Dudley No.2 canal passes underneath Gosty Hill, Halesowen, in the West Midlands.

GREGORY

Cromford Canal
69 m (76 yds) – Completed by William Jessop in 1792
Not navigable – with towpath

▲ *The west portal*

Along with Hag and Buckland Hollow, Gregory is a forgotten tunnel on the Cromford canal, overshadowed by its huge, if derelict, neighbour at Butterley. The Cromford canal, with Sir Richard Arkwright as company chairman and William Jessop as chief engineer began with high expectations of success, but these were soon tempered by problems with money, geology and engineering. However, Jessop's team included many talented individuals, with fellow engineers Benjamin Outram and Thomas Dadford senior, while Thomas Kearsley and Thomas Roundford acted as contractors.

Gregory itself does not appear to have presented any serious headaches, and was finished in 1792. It was, after all, a relatively modest undertaking of around 76 yards length; the fate of the canal hung on the far more ambitious project at Butterley; whose final collapse in 1907 (together with fierce competition with the nearby railway built in the 1830s) ultimately decided the canal's fate. Most of the Cromford was abandoned in 1944.

Gregory remains readily accessible to fit walkers, with rewarding views of the Derbyshire countryside and the spectacular Lea Wood Engine House nearby. The visitor will find the towpaths very busy during good weather. It is advisable to use High Peak Junction as a base for exploration, not least because of the availability of drinks sold by the friendly staff at the Tourist Information shop by the canal! Hazards to be aware of around Gregory include disguised canal banks and speeding mountain bikers.

▲ *The east portal*

Gregory tunnel is located on the disused Cromford canal between Cromford and Whatstandwell in Derbyshire. Visitors to the tunnel must be prepared for a long walk from High Peak Junction.

GREYWELL

Basingstoke Canal
1,125 m (1,230 yds) – Completed by William Jessop in 1794
Closed – no towpath

Basingstoke canal was built to facilitate easier movement of local agricultural produce to London markets. Plans for a six-mile loop around Greywell Hill were baulked by a local landowner, Lord Tylney, and thus a tunnel became necessary. In 1788 the chief engineer, William Jessop put his contractor, John Pinkerton, to work. In the event, although 32 miles of the canal was open by 1792, Greywell tunnel was not completed for another two years.

Rightly or wrongly, Pinkerton had acquired a reputation for sloppy work and drunkeness, which the problems encountered at Greywell tunnel tend to confirm. The canal itself never really enjoyed the level of usage anticipated, and the eagerness of shareholders to offload their burden resulted in a bewildering series of takeovers. The canal enjoyed a brief period of stability under Alec Harmsworth during the 1920s, but a distastrous collapse inside Greywell tunnel in 1932 cut the waterway in half. Dereliction followed.

From 1966 enthusiasts have worked to restore the Basingstoke. The east portal of Greywell itself was restored in 1975, under the auspices of the Basingstoke Canal Authority. The canal was re-opened up to Greywell in 1991. Since then, however, controversy has reigned between boaters

▲ *The east portal*

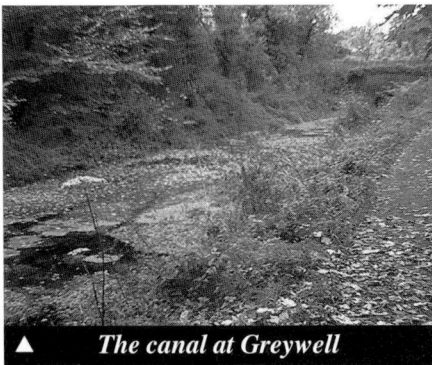
▲ *The canal at Greywell*

and nature enthusiasts. The tunnel is now home to over 12,500 bats -the largest known colony in Britain - and is an official Site of Special Scientific Interest. This, and the fact that the western portal is now apparently little better than a hole in the ground, hidden in dense woodland, suggests that Greywell tunnel is unlikely ever to re-open.

Greywell lies a few miles south-east of Basingstoke, just south of the A30 and Junction 5 of the M3.

HAG

Cromford Canal
85 m (93 yds) – Completed by William Jessop circa 1794
Abandoned 1944 – there was once a towpath

Hag was one of four tunnels on the Cromford canal, the others being Butterley, Gregory and Buckland Hollow.

The famous Richard Arkwright was company chairman of the new project (although he did not live to see its completion), with the equally renowned William Jessop as chief engineer. The Cromford had a difficult birth, and Jessop was beset with numerous problems to do with finance, engineering and geology.

When the canal eventually opened in 1794, it enjoyed a brief period of prosperity, carrying coal from East Midland fields. Hag, at 93 yards, was the second longest of the Cromford tunnels. In 1831 serious competition arrived in the shape of a railway, and canal traffic began to decline. Ironically, the railway engineer responsible was none other than Josias Jessop - the son of William Jessop.

The final collapse of Butterley tunnel in 1907 cut the canal in half, and it quickly fell into dereliction. Today, whole stretches have disappeared, and two of the tunnels, Hag and Buckland, are all but forgotten.

The site of Hag tunnel lies somewhere along the overgrown section of the Cromford canal, between Ambergate in Derbyshire and Butterley tunnel.

HARDHAM

Arun Navigation
343 m (375 yds) – Opened 1790 – Closed 1889

By 1785, the River Arun had been used by traders for over one thousand years - and all presumably found themselves inconvenienced by a three-mile loop in the river near Pulborough. Consequently, between 1785 and 1787, plans were laid to cut a short canal through the Sussex countryside between Coldwaltham and Stopham.

The largest obstacle to progress was Hardham Hill, which was overcome by a 375-yard tunnel. As soon as Hardham tunnel opened in 1790, a busy traffic in brick and chalk began.

This prosperity lasted for almost a century; but the speed of railway carriage gradually stole profitable clients from the boatmen of the Arun Navigation and the Wey & Arun canal. The short canal had fallen into disrepair by the time Hardham tunnel was closed in 1889. The section was formally abandoned in 1896.

Although restoration work is now in progress on the river, Hardham tunnel is unlikely ever to become navigable again.

Hardham tunnel lies to the west of the town of Pulborough, in Sussex.

HARECASTLE I

Trent & Mersey Canal
2,633 m (2,880 yds) – Completed by Hugh Henshall in 1777
Closed 1918 – there was no towpath

James Brindley started work on Harecastle I on 27 June 1766. In the event, the tunnel took eleven years to build, during which time Brindley died and was replaced as chief engineer by his brother-in-law, Hugh Henshall. Harecastle had presented all manner of problems, including quicksand, hard rock outcrops, springs and even deadly methane gas. It was very narrow, much like the mining tunnels at Worsley, and during construction, side tunnels were dug to exploit seams of coal.

The public were fascinated by the new tunnel, and pleasure boats cruised through it accompanied by musical bands! Due to the narrow gauge, only single line working was possible. The three hours required to "leg" through the tunnel resulted in a bottleneck, which was only resolved by Telford's parallel tunnel in 1827. After this Harecastle I was used for southbound boats.

Steam tugs replaced the leggers in 1891, but by this time subsidence was beginning to take

▲ *Harecastle I north portal*

its toll. Harecastle I became increasingly unstable until the canal authorities closed it to traffic in 1918. A collapse in 1960 finally sealed the fate of Brindley's tunnel. Today, it remains, barred and blocked - a picturesque curio beside the busy working tunnel built by Telford.

▲ *The south portals (Harecastle I on far left of picture)*

The south portals of Harecastle I & II are located just north west of Tunstall, Stoke-on-Trent. The north portals are a short walk from Kidsgrove railway station and the Harecastle pub.

HARECASTLE II
Trent & Mersey Canal
2,676 m (2,926 yds) – Completed by Thomas Telford in 1827
Fully navigable (timing restrictions) – towpath removed circa 1918

▲ *Harecastle II north portal*

In marked contrast to Harecastle I, Thomas Telford took only two years to build the new tunnel. Straighter and more stable than its predessessor, Harecastle II demonstrated the technological progress that had been made since Brindley's time.

Once Harecastle II opened in 1827, dual working was introduced. Horses pulled northbound boats through the new tunnel while southbound boats were still legged through the old one. To reduce delays, an electric tug was introduced in 1904, which consisted of two barges (one with electric motors, the other carrying 18 tons of batteries) pulling themselves along a cable on the canal bed. Later, overhead wires supplied the electricity, but these were removed in 1954.

In 1918 Harecastle I was closed due to subsidence, and single-line working ensued. Over time Harecastle II's towpath began to subside, becoming increasingly hazardous to men and horses. The increasing use of self propelled craft allowed the towpath to be removed and a pumping station was built at the south portal with a fan to extract fumes.

A door is drawn across the south portal to help the fan; this increases the sense of isolation created by the tunnel and must encourage Harecastle's various apparitions, not least the original "Kit Crewbucket" ghost. Apart from the supernatural, the most striking apsect of Harecastle is the remarkable orange hue of the water. This is a product of the local geology, rather than any man-made pollution.

▲ *Harecastle II – south portal*

The south portals of Harecastle I & II are located just north west of Tunstall, Stoke-on-Trent. The north portals are a short walk from Kidsgrove railway station and "The Harecastle" pub.

HINCASTER

Lancaster Canal
347 m (380 yds) – Completed John Fletcher & William Crossley in 1817
Abandoned 1955 – no towpath

Work on the ambitious Lancaster canal project began in 1793, under the auspices of John Rennie and his resident engineer, Archibald Millar. There were, however, numerous delays, and the northern section of the Lancaster, including Hincaster tunnel, was not opened until 18 June 1819. The new tunnel was 380 yards long, but lacking a towpath, vessels were pulled through by means of a rope fixed to the tunnel wall. The lining within both portals appears to suggest that the tunnel is stone-lined, but once within the dark recesses of the construction this changes to a cheaper brick!

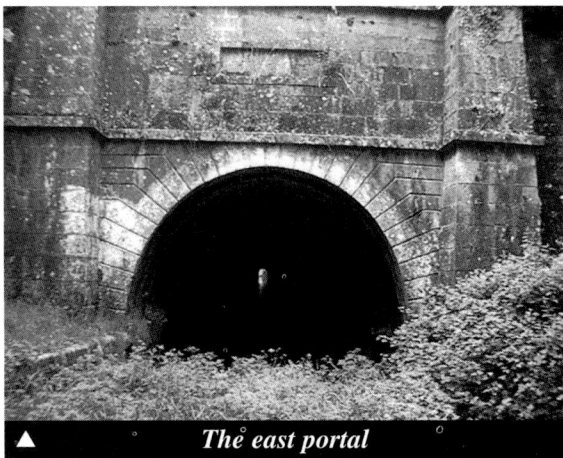

The east portal

The Tewitfield to Kendal stretch had a brief period of prosperity, until the coming of the railways in the 1830s. In 1944, the threat of total closure was fought off, but trade north of Lancaster was already in a precarious state. In 1955 the canal north of Stainton was closed and is now largely dry.

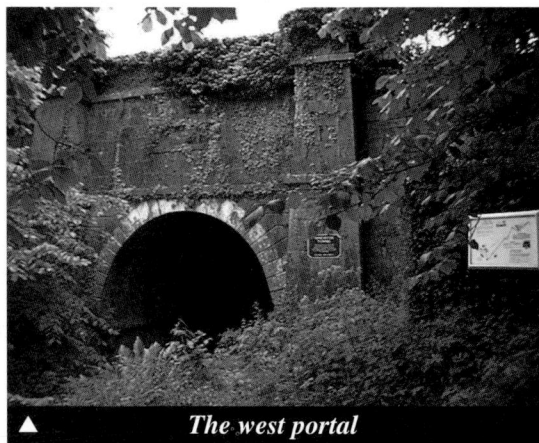

The west portal

The Lancaster Canal Trust, formed in 1963, and the Northern Reaches Restoration Group (formed in 1990) continue to make strenuous efforts to revive the northern section of the canal. It was largely through the offices of the LCT that the Royal Engineers were persuaded to repair both portals of Hincaster tunnel in 1980. It is now a scheduled 'ancient' monument.

Hincaster lies just south of the town of Kendal in the Lake District of northern England.

HUGHES BRIDGE

Donnington Wood Canal
Length uncertain – Completed by John Gilbert circa 1775
Closed circa 1797

Hughes Bridge tunnel was located on the Donnington Wood canal, near Lilleshall in Shropshire. The line was a tub-boat canal of some five and a half miles length. The brothers John Gilbert and Thomas Gilbert supervised the work, sponsored by Lord Gower. Gower was not only an influential local landowner, but brother-in-law of the "Canal Duke" of Bridgewater. Donnington Wood canal may have been in use as early as 1768, but does not appear to have been completed until around 1775.

Hughes Bridge tunnel itself appears to have had a short life; competition from rival Shropshire canals seem to have led to its closure around 1797, although the canal was not entirely abandoned until 1904.

Hughes Bridge was located near Lilleshall, which lies just north east of the modern town of Telford.

HUSBAND'S BOSWORTH

Grand Union Canal (Leicester section)
1,066 m (1,166 yds) – Completed by Benjamin Bevan in 1813
Fully navigable – no towpath

Originally part of the Old Grand Union, the tunnel initially suffered engineering and geological problems. Many experts feel that the project was unecessary, as a small detour would have sufficed to open up the navigation more efficiently.

Husband's Bosworth tunnel was opened in 1813, a year before Crick, as the engineer Benjamin Bevan and his colleagues carved out the way to Oxford and the Thames beyond.

However, the need for frequent tunnel repairs, particularly in the 1880s, gave Husband's Bosworth an unenviable reputation as a bottleneck on the Old Grand Union canal.

Incorporated into the Grand Junction Canal in 1894, the tunnel became part of the wider Grand Union (Leicester Section) in 1932. With no towpath through the tunnel, legging continued until 1939. Although the old horse path is now overgrown in parts, walkers can still follow the line from one end of the tunnel to the other.

▲ *The northeast portal*

The runs to the north of the Leicestershire village of the same name. Footpath access is via the A5199.

HYDE BANK

Peak Forest Canal
282 m (308 yds) – Completed by Benjamin Outram circa 1799
Fully navigable – no towpath

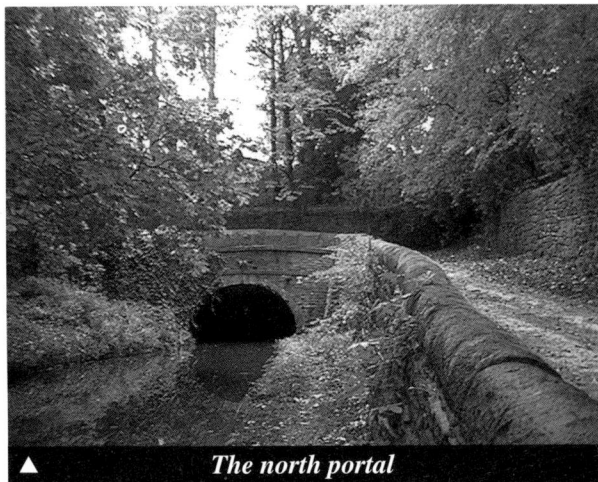

The north portal

Benjamin Outram, had possibly gained his appointment due to his association with William Jessop on the Cromford canal. Samuel Oldknow, the main sponsor of the Peak Forest, was a close associate of the Arkwright family. Outram and his resident engineer endured constant meddling, not only from their employers but from an amateur engineer called Fulton. Hyde Bank and Rose Hill were apparently built when the struggle was at its height.

Work had begun on the canal soon after it had been authorised by an Act of 1794. After the Peak Forest canal had finally been completed (c.1800), it enjoyed a lengthy period of prosperity, carrying coal, limestone and textiles. The construction of a railway line in 1838 began a slow decline, although even after purchasing the canal, the railway company operated a fleet of narrow boats until 1892.

The dearth of commercial traffic by 1958, and a disastrous breach at Marple in 1962 appeared to have sealed the canal's fate. Happily, sterling efforts by canal enthusiasts pursuaded the authorities to save the waterway, and a fully restored canal, including Hyde Bank, re-opened as part of the Cheshire Ring in March 1974. The setting around the tunnel is heavily wooded, and the south portal opens out on to a spectacular ledge.

Hyde Bank lies on the outskirts of Romiley, within the eastern boundary of Greater Manchester

ILMINSTER

Chard Canal
274 m (300 yds) – Completed by Sydney Hall in 1842 – Closed 1868

The Chard canal was surveyed by James Green and work began in 1834. Illminster was reached in 1841, and the line open through to Chard in the following year. Despite the canal's success in carrying coal, the company were no match for the burgeoning railways, which resulted in closure in 1868. The tunnel is no longer publicly accessible.

ISLINGTON

Regent's Canal (Grand Union)
878 m (960 yds) – Completed by James Morgan in 1818 (Opened 1820)
Fully navigable – no towpath

▲ **The east portal**

Horse-drawn rail waggons were used in excavating Islington tunnel, carrying away the spoil down the dry bed of the canal. The tunnel itself was completed by James Morgan and his contractor James Tate (Thomas Telford also acted as a consultant) late in 1818, but it was not officially opened until August 1820. An aquatint of 1822, two years after, shows a tree-less landscape in an industrialised area.

Initially vessels appear to have been poled or legged through by their crews, but long queues of boats and barges brought revolutionary methods to speed up navigation. In 1826 Islington became one of the first tunnels to operate a powered tug to pull craft through. The steam-engine of this tug, which wound along a chain laid on the canal bed, was efficient but extremely dirty; boatmen risked sickness and suffocation as thick smoke and choking fumes filled the tunnel - and nicknamed it "Hell".

Disaster struck in 1880 when the Islington tug sank, but at least the coke-burning replacements were markedly more pleasant. Diesel tugs were introduced in the 1930s. Today, self-powered narrowboats have made such facilities obselete.

Today, Islington remains as busy as ever, with constant traffic on the canal and towpath. The tunnel has recently benefited from extensive repair work, carried out in Spring 2000.

▲ **The west portal**

Located in central London, the east portal of Islington tunnel is a short walk from Angel tube station. The west portal lies just off Caledonian Road, northeast of King's Cross and St Pancras railway stations.

KETLEY

Ketley Canal
18 + 36 m (20 + 40 yds) – Completed by William Reynolds circa 1799
Abandoned circa 1818

Ketley canal itself was conceived as a link between the coal and ironstone mines at Ketley, Shropshire, and the metalworks at Oakengates. A prominent local entrepreneur, William Reynolds, was the leading promoter of the project and apparently appointed himself chief engineer into the bargain. By 1788 he had two to three hundred men at work on the line. Ketley was a tub-boat tunnel, split into two lengths of 20 and 40 yards respectively. Ketley Canal was always intended to be a branch of a larger Shropshire waterway, but the decline of canal traffic led to its abandonment by 1818.

The site of Ketley lies a short distance to the south-east of the centre of modern Telford.

LAPAL

Dudley No.2 Canal (later BCN)
3,470 m (3,795 yds) – Completed by William Underhill in 1798
Collapsed 1917 – there was no towpath

Lapal tunnel was perhaps the most important element of the proposal to link Dudley No 1 canal with the Worcester & Birmingham at Selly Oak (bypassing the tolls of the rival BCN). Under the original plans for Dudley No 2, Lapal was intended to measure 3,330 yards, but it eventually extended to 3,795 yards.

Josiah Clowes was appointed chief engineer of the new canal at the outset of work in 1794. Sadly, Clowes died a year later, and his assistant William Underhill was soon overwhelmed by the task. His employers then divided the workload between Underhill and Benjamin Timmins. This helped matters but could not lessen the problems encourtered at Lapal. Almost every one of the thirty shafts sunk filled with water, and quicksand ran through most of the tunnel. Despite these problems, the line opened on 28 May 1798.

Lapal proved as exhausting to maintain as it had been to build, particularly for the long-suffering superintentent of works, Thomas Green. Subsidence twice led to closure, firstly in 1801, and then in 1805 when it was closed for four months. In 1841 Green's successor, Thomas Brewin, improved the speed of traffic through the tunnel by installing a steam pumping engine near one portal, which created a current to push traffic through. It operated until 1914. Three years later Lapal suffered an extensive collapse, never to re-open. Over the last eighty years, both portals and most other traces of the tunnel have disappeared. The stretch of Lapal tunnel that lies under the modern M5 motorway is filled with concrete for safety reasons.

The site of the long-abandoned Lapal (or Lappall) tunnel lies between Halesowen and Selly Oak, just south of Birmingham.

LEEK

Caldon Canal (Leek branch)
119 m (130 yds) – Completed by John Rennie circa 1802
Fully navigable – no towpath

Early interest in extending the Caldon canal to Leek was not acted on for years, but eventually John Rennie was commissioned to supervise a new branch. Leek tunnel, an important link in this new chain, involved laborious digging through solid sandstone. Once a way had been hacked through and the tunnel completed, the Leek branch was opened in 1802.

Prosperity followed, but when water-borne traffic began to decline Leek branch was the first section of the Caldon to suffer. The coal trade had dried up several years earlier when finally the branch was officially abandoned in 1944. It was declared un-navigable in 1948. Unlike the Froghall stretch, Leek branch lacked continuing usefulness as a water supply for the Trent & Mersey, and was only saved by the determined efforts of local councils and canal enthusiasts.

Navigation was revived as far up the Caldon as Leek tunnel in 1974, and the tunnel itself was

▲ *The west portal*

restored in 1984. On 3 April 1985, Sir Leslie Young, then chairman of the British Waterways Board, unveiled a plaque to commemorate the re-opened tunnel. Today, the area around Leek tunnel is well maintained by the combined efforts of the BWB and the Staffordshire Moorlands District Council.

Both portals of Leek tunnel are located at the end of 3/4 mile walk along the towpath from the Ladderedge country park. Ladderedge is south of Leek, Staffordshire.

LILLESDON

Chard Canal
287 m (314 yds) – Completed by Syndey Hall circa 1839 – Closed 1868

Like its giant neighbour at Crimson Hill, Lillesdon was completed in the first phase of the Chard's construction between 1835 and 1839. Although a busy trade soon developed, the canal was taken over by the Bristol & Exeter Railway Company and closed in 1868.

MAIDA HILL

Regent's Canal (Grand Union)
248 m (272 yds) – Completed by John Morgan circa 1816
Fully navigable – no towpath

Part of the ambitious, and highly successful Regent's Canal scheme, Maida Hill tunnel was completed around 1816. The canal ran through land that Thomas Lord was planning to develop as a cricket ground. The canal company paid Lord £4,000 for the site, and gave the tunnelling spoil as top-soil for Lord's resited cricket ground nearby.

During a particularly cold spell in February 1855 the canal through Maida Hill froze over completely, and skaters raced each other noisily through the darkness of the tunnel. The authorities placed policemen at both portals to stop the activity, but they were soon withdrawn after angry protests from locals and skaters. Amazingly, there appear to have been no serious accidents.

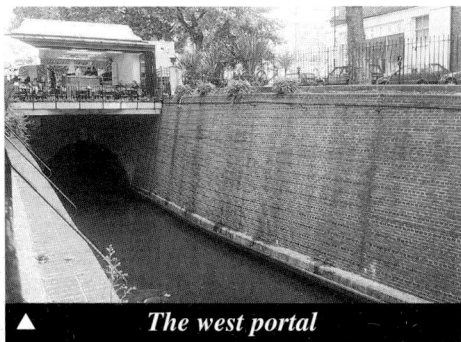

▲ **The west portal**

Maida Hill tunnel is located in central London, approximately one mile west of Regent's Park. The west portal is off the Edgware Road (A5), while the east portal is near Lisson Grove Bridge on the B507.

MANCHESTER

Manchester & Salford Junction Canal
456 m (499 yds) – Opened 1839 – Abandoned 1922

The Manchester & Salford Junction canal was opened in 1839, linking the Rochdale canal with the Irwell Navigation and Manchester, Bolton & Bury canal. The link canal ceased to carry much commercial traffic after the 1870s. During World War II the tunnel was used as an air raid shelter, but it has now disappeared under urban development.

The site of Manchester tunnel lies slightly to the north-west of the city centre.

MORWELLDOWN

Tavistock Canal
2,322 m (2,540 yds) – Opened in 1816 – Not navigable – no towpath

Morwelldown tunnel was one of the longest of its time, and took no less than thirteen years to complete. It now functions as a water supply to a generating station. The southern portal lies within Morwellham Open Air Museum.

Morwelldown tunnel lies about three miles south-west of Tavistock, Devon.

NETHERTON

Dudley No. 2 Canal
2,768 m (3,027 yds) – Completed in 1858
Fully navigable – with double towpath

The Dudley Canal Company first planned Netherton as an alternative to Dudley tunnel in 1792. However, when the company built Dudley No2 canal, the project was shelved, and Dudley was instead circumvented by a long route through Gosty Hill and Lapal tunnels to join the Worcester & Birmingham canal.

Dudley's continuing traffic congestion, and the time-consuming alternative meant that a Netherton tunnel remained a good proposition even after railways began to erode canal income. The idea was revived in 1813 when the BCN proposed a merger with its Dudley rivals. It was not until 1855, however, that Netherton was finally authorised, with the first sod being turned by Lord Ward on the very last day of that year. The tunnel opened on 20 August 1858.

▲ *Inside the tunnel*

As the last significant canal tunnel to be built during the Industrial Revolution, Netherton's construction benefited from the huge improvements which had been made in civil engineering during the years of "canal mania". In contrast to earlier tunnels of a similar size, which had usually taken more than a decade to complete, Netherton took less than three years. The tunnel featured towpaths on both sides, as well as generous width and headroom. Gas lighting (later electric) enabled 24-hour passage. The £302,000 spent on Netherton's construction was soon recouped, and investors rewarded with good dividends. The tunnel has remained open since its inception, save for major invert replacement work in the early 1980s.

Although parallel to Dudley tunnel, Netherton is at a lower level having branched from Telford's BCN line. Netherton is also shorter than Dudley due to the steep cuttings leading to its entrances. Despite its length and darkness, it is now totally unlit.

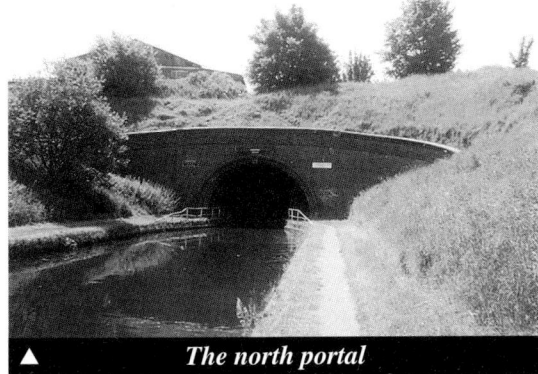

▲ *The north portal*

Netherton lies to the west of Birmingham, parallel to Dudley tunnel.

NEWBOLD (OLD)

Oxford Canal
114 m (125 yds) – Completed by Samuel Simcock in 1774
Sealed 1834 – there was a towpath

The long-abandoned south portal

Part of the Oxford canal, begun around 1770, the original tunnel completed at Newbold in 1774 was 125 yds long and 12 foot 6 inches wide. This waterway meandered with quaint inefficiency through the Midlands countryside - in part due to the need for the engineers, James Brindley and Samuel Simcock, to avoid the property of an unco-operative landowner.

Following Brindley's death in 1772, it was left to Simcock to complete the project. The tortuous looped canal lasted almost sixty years until Victorian engineers straightened the route. As a consequence the old tunnel at Newbold was cut off and sealed. It remains today only as a bricked-up portal, standing forlorn and forgotten in an overgrown corner by St Botolph's churchyard.

The remains of the original eighteenth-century tunnel at Newbold lie beside St Botolph's church a few hundred yards up the hill from "The Boat" pub.

NEWBOLD (NEW)

Oxford Canal
229 m (250 yds) – Completed by Sir William Cubitt in 1834
Fully navigable – with double towpath

In 1834, the cost-conscious Victorians rationalised the meandering stretch of the Oxford canal between Coventry and Rugby. In cutting this straighter route, William Cubitt and his associate, Mr Vignoles, discarded fourteen miles of canal, including the existing eighteenth-century tunnels at Newbold and Wolfhampcote.

The new tunnel, constructed almost at right angles to the old, was exactly twice as long, with a towpath down each side. At around 15 ft beam, it was slightly wider than the old tunnel of Brindley and Simcock.

The south portal

The north portal

Today, it remains a bustling waterway, with craft bearing names of towns as far away as Hull and Guildford. Within yards of the south portal stand the equally busy *Boat* and *Barley Mow* pubs.

The double towpath is still accessible, although there are deep puddles in several places.

The 1834 tunnel can be found on the northern tip of Newbold village, just north west of Rugby in Warwickshire.

93

NEWNHAM

Kington, Leominster & Stourport Canal
86 m (94 yds) – Completed by Thomas Dadford junior in 1794
Closed 1858

The construction of the Kington, Leominster & Stourport canal was only loosely supervised by its overworked engineer Thomas Dadford junior. For this and other reasons the Leominster proved an unmitigated disaster; large stretches of the canal, including most of its tunnels, were never completed.

Compared with Pensax and Southnet, Newnham was a minnow of 94 yards length, but it was actually opened and used commercially. Ironically, the tunnel was not part of Dadford's original plan; he had intended a cutting instead. John Rennie, called in to report on the Leominster tunnels, was scathing of the quality of engineering - his criticisms largely borne out by the fact that Newnham suffered a collapse.

Abandoned with the rest of the canal in 1858, Newnham has been filled in. Both portals appear to have been destroyed sometime in the 1970s.

The site of Newnham tunnels lies hidden close to the A456 north-east of Tenbury Wells on the border between Worcestershire and Shropshire.

NEWPORT

Monmouthshire Canal
128 m (140 yds) – Completed by Thomas Dadford junior in 1796
Closed 1854 – towpath

Strictly speaking, the chief engineer of the Monmouthshire canal, Thomas Dadford junior, built two tunnels in Newport; one was located under Mill Street, while the other ran for 140 yds under Barrick's Hill.

The canal company succeeded in its aim of improving access from inland Wales to the coast, opening the line from Newport to Pontnewynydd in 1796, and an additional stretch to Crumlin by 1799. It was an astute move for the directors to convert their charge to a railway company in 1845, even if the change meant doom for large stretches of the waterway. In 1854 half a mile of canal was filled in through Newport, and a further stretch was closed in 1879.

Commercial traffic between Newport and Brecon ceased in 1915, and no cargoes reached Pontymoile after 1938. The Monmouthshire & Brecon (as it had become) was progressively closed by Acts of 1954 and 1962, but has now been partly re-opened for tourism.

The site of the Newport tunnels lies under the modern town centre of Newport in South Wales.

NORWOOD

Chesterfield Canal
2,836 m (3,102 yds) – Completed by Hugh Henshall in 1775
Collapsed 1908 – there was no towpath

In the Autumn of 1771 James Brindley and his resident engineer John Varley began work on Norwood tunnel, using three hundred labourers digging from both ends. Momentum was lost when Brindley died, for it was not until the summer of 1773 that the new chief engineer, Hugh Henshall, was able to devote much attention to the project. He declared the work, much of which had been contracted to John Varley's relations, to be unsatisfactory. However, Henshall was able to make good the deficiencies, and Norwood was duly completed.

▲ *The northeast portal*

The tunnel was officially opened on 9 May 1775, traversed by three vessels loaded with hundreds of sightseers and a brass band! Henshall had done his job so well that despite the great length of the tunnel, it was so straight that one could see the daylight at the opposite end.

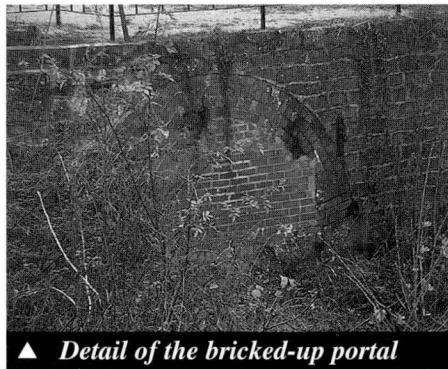

▲ *Detail of the bricked-up portal*

Problems soon emerged and mining subsidence was to prove a particular concern. As early as 1777, coal mining had weakened the arch of the tunnel roof. Tens of thousands of pounds spent on repairs were in vain; by 1904 the headroom was down to 4' 10", and in 1908 a collapse closed the tunnel for good.

There has been much activity on the part of the local society to restore the entire length of the Chesterfield canal. Any attempt to revive Norwood tunnel however, will undoubtedly prove an extremely difficult project. The east portal is bricked up, but in reasonable condition, considering that the 1908 collapse was at that end. The west end is filled where the M1 motorway crosses over the top, and the west portal itself has disappeared.

The east portal can be found at Kiveton Park, about six miles north-west of Worksop. The site of the west portal lies just under two miles to the south-east, near Killamarsh.

OAKENGATES

Shropshire Canal
Completed circa 1792
Abandoned 1857

Work started on the Shropshire canal in 1788, under the supervision of John Lowdon. It was a tub-boat canal, which linked with the Ketley canal of William Reynolds and the Donnington Wood canal. The canal had very influential backing, not only from Reynolds and local business interests, but from the Gilbert brothers and William Jessop. Oakengates, under the London - Holyhead road, was the shortest of three tunnels on the canal (the others being Snedshill and Stirchley), and lay close to the junction with the Ketley canal. The stretch between Wrockwardine Wood and the Windmill Inclined Plane was abandoned in 1857, and traffic ceased a year later. The collapse of Snedshill in July 1855 may have influenced the decision to close the section and with it Oakengates.

The site of Oakengates tunnel lies close to the west of the modern town centre of Telford.

OCKER HILL

Birmingham Canal Navigations
Completed circa 1772
Now closed

Ocker Hill lies on a junction between the historical Birmingham Canal Navigations and the Walsall Canal. This short tunnel was located near Tipton, West Midlands. It was only ever used to transfer water to the higher "Wolverhampton" level of the canal.

PENSAX

Kington, Leominster & Stourport Canal
Planned at 3,519 m (3,850 yd) – Left incomplete circa 1796
Canal formally abandoned 1858

Pensax would have been the longest canal tunnel of its day - had it ever been completed. Coal was the principal reason for the grandly-named Kington, Leominster & Stourport canal, but sadly, it was never moved by the waterway, and continued to be drawn overland.

Thomas Dadford junior, the Leominster's engineer, had clearly taken on too many commissions, and was unable to supervise the construction of the canal properly. John Rennie, reporting on the structure of the canal, was critical of its tunnels. Work on Pensax ceased as the canal company ran out of money and all hope of completion was dead long before the ill-fated canal was finally closed in 1858.

The site of Pensax tunnel lies a few miles south-west of Stourport, Worcestershire.

OXENHALL

Herefordshire & Gloucestershire Canal
2,004 m (2,192 yds) – Completed by Robert Whitworth circa 1798
Under restoration – no towpath

TheHerefordshire & Gloucestershire canal was built in two distinct stages and took over fifty years to build. The first section from Over (Gloucester) to Ledbury, which contains Oxenhall tunnel, was constructed between 1793 and 1798. Work began under the supervision of Josiah Clowes, but following his death the canal company brought in the ubiquitous troubleshooter Robert Whitworth. The section between Ledbury and Hereford was begun in 1839 and completed in 1845.

Oxenhall tunnel was one of the longest tunnels built during the canal era. Construction was not easy. Twenty shafts were sunk to build the tunnel and extensive problems with water at the workings were encountered. The use of horsepower to remove the water proved insufficient and so expensive steam engines were employed instead. The high cost of the first phase to Ledbury meant that the second phase to Hereford had to be delayed. The complete canal did not enjoy a long life: Oxenhall was closed in 1881.

The south portal

The north portal

During the 1990's the Herefordshire & Gloucestershire Canal Trust began restoration on both the canal and Oxenhall tunnel. The area leading to the south portal has been worked upon, and the portal brickwork has been rebuilt. The "Boyce Court" (north) portal is almost totally submerged in sediment and most of the brickwork has collapsed. It is over-washed by a stream.

Located just to the north of Newent in Gloucestershire, the tunnel now lies under the M50.

PRESTON BROOK

Trent & Mersey Canal
1,136 m (1,242 yds) – Completed by Hugh Henshall in 1775
Fully navigable – no towpath

After James Brindley's death, his brother-in-law, Hugh Henshall, completed the link between the Trent and the Mersey. Unlike Saltersford and Barnton the need for a tunnel had already been anticipated at Preston Brook. It was completed in 1775 - two years before the canal was opened along its complete length.

The north portal

The three tunnels were at that time the longest and most ambitious attempted, although the Duke of Bridgewater was dissatisfied to find that his larger barges could not pass through them. Tugs were introduced in the nineteenth century to speed traffic through the bottlenecks; but even in these self-powered days, the narrowness and crookedness of Preston Brook still presents some problems. Movement through the tunnel in both directions is subject to careful regulation; access restricted to specific periods for both northbound and southbound traffic.

Preston's most spectacular collapse once closed a post office which perched over the centre of the tunnel. However, following extensive repairs in the 1980s it is now in good condition. Mementos of the re-opening ceremony (17 April 1984) remain in the form of plaques placed by the BWB and the very active Trent & Mersey Canal Society on either side of the north portal. The old horse route remains, providing the walker with a path from one portal to the other.

Preston Brook lies a few miles south-east of Runcorn in Cheshire

PUTNAL FIELDS
Kington, Leominster & Stourport Canal
119 m (130 yds) – Completed by Thomas Dadford junior in 1796
Formally abandoned in 1858

Putnal Fields tunnel was one of the few tunnels on the ill-fated Kington, Leominster & Stourport canal actually to see commercial use. Even though it was nowhere near the length of other planned Leominster tunnels such as Southnet and Pensax, the 130 yards of Putnal Fields tunnel presented the engineer, Thomas Dadford junior, with several difficulties. Delays in Putnal's construction held up the opening of the surrounding canal for over two years - and thus contributed to the acute financial problems of the canal company.

▲ *The northeast portal*

John Rennie, brought in to report on the structure of the canal, was highly critical of Dadford's tunnels. The closure of the Leominster in 1858 meant abandonment and dereliction for Putnal Fields.

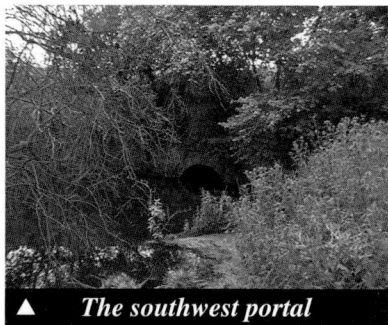

▲ *The southwest portal*

The portals lie either side of the B4362, close to the junction of the A49 and A456 in Shropshire.

ROMFORD
Romford Canal
Length uncertain – Begun in 1875
Aborted in 1877

Although the Romford canal was a short and obscure chapter in the history of British inland waterways, it did produce one tunnel! After several attempts, an Act authorising the Romford canal was passed in 1875, and work started immediately not only on a lock but on a tunnel underneath the London, Tilbury & Southend railway. However, the age of canals had long since passed, and it was no surprise that the project was aborted in 1877. The Romford Canal Company was liquidated in 1910.

The site of the tunnel was later incorporated into the London Underground District Line to Upminster, suggesting that its location would have been somewhere between West Ham and Hornchurch.

ROSE HILL

Peak Forest Canal
91 m (100 yd) – Completed by Benjamin Outram circa 1799
Fully navigable (now opened out) – there was a towpath

The chief engineer of the Peak Forest canal, Benjamin Outram, had possibly gained his appointment because of his association with William Jessop on the Cromford canal. Samuel Oldknow, the main sponsor of the Peak Forest, was a close associate of the Arkwright family near Cromford. Despite this, Outram and his resident engineer endured constant meddling, not only from their employers but from an amateur engineer called Fulton. Rose Hill and neighbouring Hyde Bank were apparently built when this power struggle was at its height; by the time   was dug, however, Outram had prevailed.

Work had begun on the canal soon after it had been authorised by an Act of 1794. After the Peak Forest canal had finally been completed (c.1800), it enjoyed a lengthy period of prosperity, carrying coal, limestone and textiles. The construction of a railway line in 1838 began a slow decline, although after purchasing the canal, the railway company continued to operate a fleet of narrow boats until 1892.

The site of the east portal

The dearth of commercial traffic by 1958, and a disastrous breach at Marple, near Rose Hill, in 1962 appeared to have sealed the canal's fate. Happily, sterling efforts by canal enthusiasts pursuaded the authorities to save the waterway, and a fully restored canal re-opened as part of the Cheshire Ring in March 1974. Rose Hill tunnel was opened up to the sky at some point in the nineteenth century, and the remains of the east portal have been incorporated into the bridge which presently occupies the site.

Rose Hill (now only extant as a bridge and a narrow channel) and the neighbouring tunnel of Hyde Bank are a short distance to the north of Marple, now within the boundary of Greater Manchester

SADDINGTON

Grand Union Canal (Leicester Section)
805 m (880 yds) – Completed by William Jessop in 1797
Fully navigable – no towpath

The Leicestershire & Northamptonshire Union canal was approved by Act of Parliament in 1791, and begun soon after under the aegis of chief engineer William Jessop. Day-to-day operations were supervised by John Varley and William Fletcher. The first phase of the canal was completed in 1794, before work began on Saddington tunnel.

Tunnelling in the area proved extremely difficult, and several contactors tried and failed before Saddington tunnel was finally completed in 1797. Quicksands had caused several cave-ins, not only in the tunnel itself, but also in the cutting leading to the entrance. Perhaps because of the many abortive attempts, Fletcher found the tunnel to be crooked and John Varley was forced to foot the bill for repairs!

The south portal

In common with the other tunnels on the Leicester stretch (the L & NUC was absorbed by the Grand Junction canal in 1894), Crick and Husband's Bosworth, there is no towpath through the tunnel, and so consequently legging continued until 1939. Despite the lack of a towpath, there are well-trodden towpaths at either portal, and an excellent footpath over the tunnel itself, which follows the old horse route.

Vicious weather during the winter of 1978-79 caused the tunnel to be closed for a period, but it appears today to be in reasonable condition. The tunnel apparently contains a family of bats, who share their home with a resident ghost in the shape of a headless lady.

The north portal

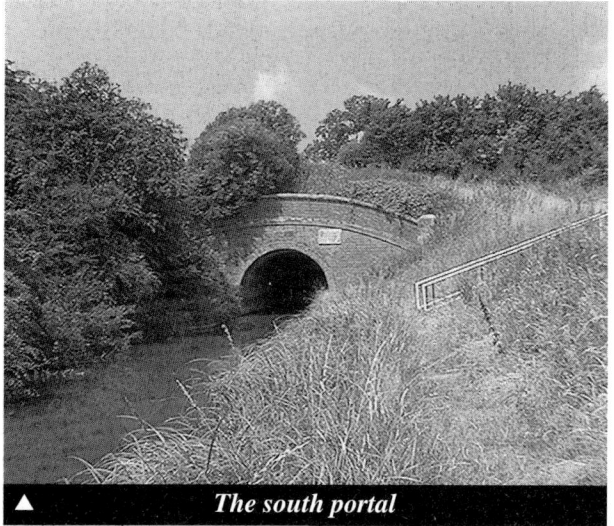

The northern portal can be found 1/2 mile south east of the village of Fleckney in Leicestershire. The southern portal is located just north of Bridge 72, half-way between Saddington and Smeeton Westaby

SALTERSFORD

Trent & Mersey Canal
388 m (424 yds) – Completed by Hugh Henshall in 1777
Fully navigable – no towpath

Following his brother-in-law's death in 1772, Hugh Henshall took over from Brindley as Chief Engineer of the Trent & Mersey. He found canal construction through Cheshire no easy task, and in addition to the expected tunnel at Preston Brook was forced to dig two tunnels near Barnton. These were Barnton itself and Saltersford.

The south portal

All three tunnels (at the time the most ambitious then attempted) are built to the narrow gauge, although the canal itself is wide along this stretch. The laborious task of legging boats through the tunnels made all three bottlenecks to canal traffic. This congestion was eased slightly when steam tugs were introduced in the nineteenth century. The tugs on the three tunnels had revolving wheels, which acted as fenders and protected the vessels during collisions with the tunnel lining.

In common with a number of Trent & Mersey canal tunnels, Saltersford underwent extensive renovation during the early 1980s. A plaque commemorates its re-opening on 17 April 1984 by Sir Frank Price, then Chairman of the British Waterways Board.

Walkers taking the path over the tunnel once used by the horses will encounter near the north end a mile post peculiar to the Trent & Mersey, reading "Shardlow 83 / Preston Brook 5"

The tunnel lies just north west of the village of Barnton, between Runcorn and Northwich in Cheshire.

SAPPERTON

Thames & Severn Canal
3,490 m (3,817 yds) – Completed by Robert Whitworth in 1789
Closed – no towpath

▲ *Coates portal*

At the time of its inception in 1784 Sapperton was the longest and largest tunnel then built. The tunnel forms part of the summit pound of the Thames & Severn canal, along which cloth was shipped from Cotswold mills to London and Bristol. In contrast with contemporary tunnels such as Harecastle, Sapperton was designed from the outset to be a full 15' wide. Despite geological problems and doubts of many experts, the company succeeded with their plan. A total of 25 shafts were sunk in the five years it took to construct the tunnel. Robert Whitworth, the chief engineer, generously gave credit for the tunnel to his assistant Josiah Clowes. The success of the tunnel helped Clowes revive a flagging career. Charles Jones was initially engaged as contractor for the tunnel, but because of drunken incompetence, he was replaced by John Nock & Ralph Sheppard. The first boat navigated through the tunnel in April 1789. It remained open until around 1894.

The Great Western Railway tried repeatedly to rent the tunnel, intending to convert it to railway use. When Sapperton finally fell into the GWR's hands around 1895, vociferous protests led to the passing of an Act, transferring ownership to a trust formed by the local authorities and interested canal companies. In 1901, ownership was transferred to Gloucester County Council. The Council undertook extensive restoration of the canal which resulted in the summit pound and tunnel being re-opened in January 1904.

▲ *Daneway portal*

The Thames & Severn continued to suffer from extensive water loss as a consequence of the fissured limestone geology through which it passed, and the tunnel was often closed for long periods. The last boat passed through Sapperton in May 1911. The tunnel has suffered from collapses; the brick and stone lining being unable to support the fuller's earth and oolite structures through which it passes. Both canal and tunnel were formally abandoned in 1927. Restoration is now being undertaken by the Cotswold Canal Trust, with the goal of reopening the tunnel to navigation early in the twenty-first century. Boat trips are run from the Coates Portal into the tunnel on Sundays, December to May (subject to water levels).

The west (Daneway) portal of Sapperton tunnel is situated approximately 1/2 mile west of the Gloucestershire village. The east (Coates) portal lies about a mile to the south of Coates village.

SCOUT

Huddersfield Narrow Canal
201 m (220 yds) – Completed by Robert Whitworth circa 1799
Awaiting re-opening – with towpath

The Huddersfield Narrow canal was originally conceived as a link between the Ashton canal at Marsden and Sir John Ramsden's canal at Huddersfield itself. Benjamin Outram was appointed chief engineer, and work began in July 1794. Although Outram had been closely associated with William Jessop on the Cromford canal, he was perhaps out of his depth in a solo capacity. During a period of illness, Outram's place was taken by the vastly more experienced Robert Whitworth. Whitworth described the standard of masonry and earthworks as the worst he had ever seen.

The south portal

Whitworth's scathing comments were aimed more at Standedge tunnel further north on the canal, rather than the modest Scout. Even today, Scout is overshadowed by its massive sister tunnel. Scout tunnel along with the rest of the canal was complete by 1799, but problems over Standedge delayed the official opening of the canal until 1811, long after Outram had been succeeded by John Rooth

After almost a century and a half of operation, the Huddersfield Narrow was abandoned in 1945. The last recorded trip along the length of the canal took place three years later. The canal survived principally because of its usefulness as a water supply. Ironically the great interest and finance now being invested in Standedge tunnel has had a beneficial knock-on effect for Scout, which is now enjoying its own restoration programme.

The north portal

Scout tunnel is situated just off the A635, between Stalybridge and Mossley, on the eastern outskirts of Greater Manchester.

SELLERS YARD

Huddersfield Narrow Canal
320 m (350 yds) – Completed by Costain Ltd in 2000
Awaiting canal re-opening – no towpath

The Huddersfield Narrow canal was officially closed by Act of Parliament in 1944, and the land on which many parts of the canal stood were subsequently purchased by interested parties. One such stretch ran near the centre of Huddersfield, where the canal passed through what had become Sellers Yard factory estate. It was soon filled in.

▲ Construction at the east portal (Oct 1999)

To allow the Huddersfield Narrow to once more pass through Sellers Yard the level of the canal has been lowered and a culvert created. Until 1999 a lock remained under the A616 south of Huddersfield town centre. With the dropping of the canal, there was no need for the old lock at the east end. The tunnel has absorbed this lock and emerges on the east side of the A616. The old road bridge east parapet has thus become the east portal.

Travelling east, the canal is open to the sky for about 100 metres before entering Bates Mill tunnel. A further 500 metres from Bates Mill, the Huddersfield Narrow joins the Huddersfield Broad canal at Apsley Basin.

This brand new concrete tunnel lies under the main factory estate of Sellers Yard on the west side of the A616 southbound from Huddersfield town centre.

SHORTWOOD

Worcester & Birmingham Canal
561 m (613 yds) – Completed by Thomas Cartwright in 1807
Fully navigable – no towpath

Shortwood tunnel was completed in 1807, shortly before the Worcester & Birminghham Canal Company ran out of funds. It was three years before Shortwood's more famous neighbour, Tardebigge, was opened.

▲ *The north portal*

The company's rivals, particularly the BCN, had already placed many obstacles in the way of the new canal, leaving it with broad-gauge tunnels and narrow-gauge locks.

Like Tardebigge, no towpath was built through Shortwood tunnel, and legging was required to propel craft through. This changed in the 1870s when the tug service through Wast Hill tunnel at King's Norton was extended, and boats were towed through all three tunnels without unhitching. The tug service lasted until the early twentieth century.

Regular commercial traffic in coal and chocolate crumb (to Cadburys Bourneville factory) lasted until the early 1960s. Unlike many other canals, the Worcester & Birmingham, together with its tunnels, remained healthily busy to enjoy the modern revival of waterway traffic. One aspect of Shortwood has remained unchanged throughout its life, however; which is that boaters must be prepared to get wet when passing through!

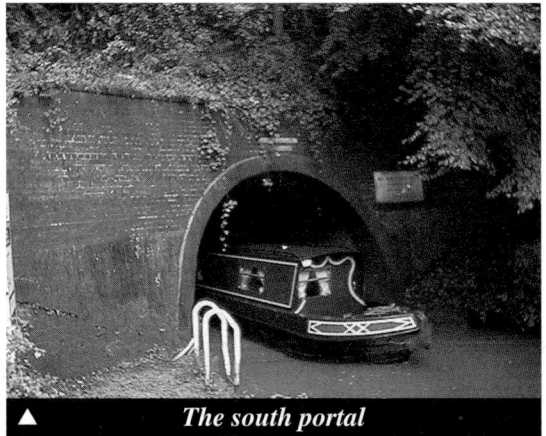

▲ *The south portal*

Shortwood tunnel is in Worcestershire, lying south west of the Birmingham suburb of Alvechurch.

SHREWLEY

Grand Union Canal
396 m (433 yds) – Completed by William Felkin in 1799
Fully navigable – no towpath

Originally built as part of the Warwick & Birmingham canal, the purpose of this stretch was to link the Black Country to the River Avon and thence to the River Severn and the sea ports of Gloucester and Bristol. Ironically, after being absorbed into the Grand Union, its principal function was to connect Birmingham with the Port of London.

The village of Shrewley presented an obstacle to the canal builders. Perched on a hill there was no way it could have been traversed by locks on either side. There was no adequate source of water available or space to build a reservoir to support the working of such locks. The engineers could not create a deep cutting, as this would have obliterated half the village.

▲ *The north portal*

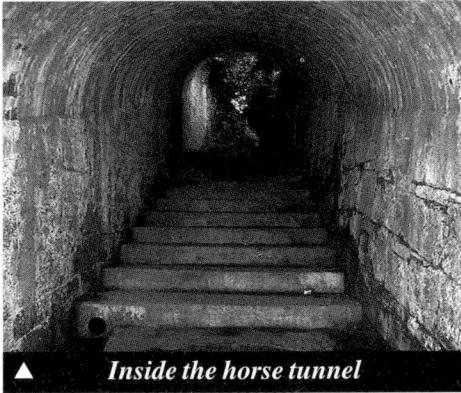

▲ *Inside the horse tunnel*

The obvious answer was a tunnel. Cuttings were made on either side of the village to minimise its length. At Shrewley's northern end geological features from the Triassic period were exposed. These features are still in place, now protected by a preservation order which prevents any future development.

As no towpath runs through the tunnel, the horses were unharnessed and led over the hill. To reduce the exertion of the steep climb a horse tunnel, 37 metres long, was soon dug near the north portal. This still forms part of the path today.

As Shrewley is notoriously wet inside, featuring a continuous stream of water from the apex of the roof at one point, waterproofs would be a wise purchase for anyone intending to boat through the tunnel.

The south portal ▶

Running directly underneath the village of Shrewley, this Warwickshire tunnel forms part of a long pound which runs from the top of the notorious Hatton Locks to Kingswood Junction.

SNARESTONE

Ashby Canal
229 m (250 yds) – Completed by Thomas Newbold in 1798
Fully navigable – no towpath

In concept, the Ashby canal, approved by an Act of 1794, must have seemed a safe investment. The plan to link the rich Derbyshire coalfields around Ashby-de-la-Zouch with the main Midlands canal network appeared relatively straightforward; the survey found no need for any locks, and just two tunnels. In a region abounding with experienced miners these were not likely to prove too difficult.

▲ **The south portal**

▲ **The north portal**

In the event only Snarestone tunnel was ever dug. The proliferation of coal mines, whilst providing great commercial potential, meant that the land beyond Moira was riddled with seams and inherrently unsafe.

The canal never reached Ashby. In the latter half of the twentieth century, even the stretch to Moira was abandoned due to problems of subsidence. Consequently, today's travellers will find that soon after traversing Snarestone tunnel the canal ends abruptly in a field.

Boaters will find consolation in the terminus facilities, with views of an ice-breaker and the spectacular Victorian Gothic waterworks - to say nothing of a good pint at the *Globe Inn* beside the tunnel. Sobriety, however, is advisable if walking along the towpath; the canal bank is obscured by reeds in several places and can be treacherous.

Snarestone tunnel runs directly under the village of Snarestone in Leicestershire. The village is approximately two miles due east of Junction 11 of the M42.

108

SNEDSHILL

Shropshire Canal
255 m (279 yds) – Completed circa 1792
Abandoned 1857

Work started on the Shropshire canal in 1788, under the supervision of John Lowdon. The canal promised to open up access to several other waterways and had influential backing from William Reynolds, William Jessop and the Gilbert brothers.

Snedshill tunnel, located within the environs of the modern town of Telford, was a substantial tunnel of some 279 yards (255 m) and stood just north of the junction between the Shropshire canal and the Ketley canal. The sister tunnel of Stirchley, and a shorter tunnel at Oakengates completed the Shropshire trio.

Snedshill appears to have experienced some geological problems during its life, particularly a bad collapse in July 1855. This incident may have influenced the canal's owners' decision to abandon the line between Wrockwardine Wood and Windmill inclined plane in 1857. Commercial traffic ceased a year later.

The site of Snedshill tunnel lay just to the west of the modern town centre of Telford.

SOUTHAMPTON

Andover Canal
Planned at 804 m (880 yds) – Begun circa 1795?
Closed circa 1808 - Probably never completed

Much confusion surrounds the long tunnel at Southampton. Had it been completed, the tunnel would have been a substantial one of some 880 yards.

Differences of opinion abound among various writers even as to the canal the tunnel was on (the Southampton & Salisbury being one suggested alternative to the Andover). Joseph Hall first surveyed the line in 1793, which may have been followed up immediately by construction work subsequently aborted around 1808.

A further attempt may have been made in the 1820s, with which Thomas Jenkins has been mentioned as a contractor. Jenkins, who was involved with the equally ill-fated Southnet on the Kington, Leominster and Stourport canal, does not seem to have made any great headway, and apart from appearing in a 1990 article by the famous tunnel hunter, John Gagg, Southampton tunnel has otherwise been forgotten and consigned to history.

The site of Southampton tunnel lies fairly close to the city centre.

SOUTHNET

Kington, Leominster & Stourport Canal
1,146 m (1,254 yds) – Completed by Thomas Dadford junior in 1795
Collapsed – no towpath

During the 'canal mania' period in the late 18th century, canals were constructed all over the country as rich landowners, manufacturers and mine-owners saw how much money was being made by the pioneers. Where there had never been an efficient means of transporting high tonnages of raw materials and goods there was suddenly a system whereby one narrowboat pulled by one horse could transport ten times the weight carried by a cart pulled by two or more horses, or a hundred times the load of a pack horse.

The east portal

The coalmine owners around Mamble and Tunbury, Sir William Blount in particular, wanted to exploit this growing transport method and had the money to invest - unwisely as it turned out - in the venture.

The east-west section of the canal from Woofferton to Marlbrook went very well, including the short Newnham tunnel. This section was in use by 1795, carrying coal to Woofferton Wharf, and Southnet was finished but remained cut off from the main waterway by about 100 metres near Wharf House where the canal ended.

Then problems began to accumulate. Delays with Putnal Fields tunnel on the north-south section south of Woofferton prevented coal reaching Leominster. Southnet tunnel collapsed near its wet eastern end. John Rennie was brought in to inspect the work in 1796. He criticised the design of the tunnel and the workmanship along with other flaws elsewhere on the canal. Dadford was blamed for inadequate supervision of Thomas Jenkins and other contractors. Bankruptcy was inevitable. Southnet was never used.

Detail

Southnet is situated near the Worcestershire / Shropshire border, between Kidderminster and Leominster.

SOWERBY BRIDGE

Rochdale Canal
39 m (43 yds) – Completed by William Jessop in 1798
Closed 1952 – there was no towpath

Curiously, in view of the fact that it was only 43 yards long, Sowerby Bridge was also known as 'Sowerby Long Tunnel'. The tunnel lay under the town centre of Sowerby Bridge, on the outskirts of Halifax, West Yorkshire.

After several attempts, thwarted by various vested interests, the Rochdale canal was finally authorised in 1794. William Jessop was appointed chief engineer, with William Crossley as resident. The northern section of canal from the junction with the Calder & Hebble, of which this tunnel was a part, was opened in 1798. Complete navigation followed in December 1804.

Like so many other canals, the Rochdale suffered severe competition from the railways, but commercial traffic survived through Sowerby until 1939. This section of the canal was officially closed in 1952, but since then sterling work by enthusiasts within the Rochdale Canal Restoration Scheme has reclaimed the section from Sowerby Bridge to Littleborough. Sadly, the tunnel was obliterated by modern building development. The revival of the Rochdale necessitated a new and longer tunnel: Tuel.

The town of Sowerby Bridge lies in the middle of a triangle between Halifax, Huddersfield and Rochdale.

STIRCHLEY

Shropshire canal
257 m (281 yds) – Completed by John Lowdon circa 1788
Destroyed 1860

Like most other canal projects in Shropshire Stirchley tunnel owed much to the backing of William Reynolds. John Lowdon was appointed as engineer, and appears to have completed Stirchley before being replaced by a series of unsuccessful engineers.

Stirchley was 281 yards long, 10ft wide and some 13ft high. The financial problems suffered first by the Shropshire canal companies, then by a union of rail and waterway interests was mercifully curtailed when the line was purchased by an aggressive railway company in 1858. The canal had already been abandoned between Wrockwardine Wood and the Windmill inclined plane, including the other Shropshire tunnels at Snedshill and Oakengates. Stirchley tunnel was destroyed soon after, when a railway was built across the site around 1860.

The site of Stirchley tunnel lies within the new town of Telford in Shropshire.

STANDEDGE

Huddersfield Narrow Canal
Final length 5,210 m (5,698 yds) – Completed by John Rooth in 1811
Scheduled to re-open April 2001 – no towpath

The longest canal tunnel ever constructed in the British Isles, Standedge was initially planned at 4,950m (5,413 yd), but was later extended to its present length. At 196 m (645 ft) above sea level, this is the highest summit pound and tunnel in the country, and the maximum depth below ground level is 183 m (600 ft), makes Standedge argueably the deepest tunnel in the UK. There are also no less than thirteen communication passages to the neighbouring railway tunnels.

▲ *The north portal*

A burst of canal building around Manchester followed the success of the Bridgewater canal, fuelled by a huge demand to transport goods across the Pennines to Yorkshire cities and east coast ports. As the Leeds & Liverpool proved a long, winding route, commercial pressure grew for a shorter canal of 19.75 miles. This required a very long tunnel in the summit pound.

The Huddersfield Narrow canal was sanctioned by Parliament in 1794. Work started under Benjamin Outram at Marsden in the April, and at Diggle some months later. However, with only picks, shovels and black-powder available for blasting through the solid millstone grit of the Pennines, Standedge tunnel took seventeen years to complete. By 1799, while the rest of the canal was complete (except the Diggle flight of locks) only 1,830 metres of tunnel had been dug, together with the fourteen shafts. Average progress was less than eleven metres per week. When a flood devastated much of the canal the company went bankrupt.

Another Act allowed extra capital to be raised in 1800. Nicholas Brown, the surveyor, was sacked and replaced by John Rooth. When Outram fell ill in 1801, Rooth effectively took over. In 1807 Thomas Telford was brought in as a consultant. His involvement resulted in the Swellands reservoir, although it burst in 1810, killing six people in the Colne Valley.

The opening of the Huddersfield Narrow canal, virtually complete by late 1810, was delayed by the floods. In April 1811 a grand opening ceremony finally took place at Diggle, with a band, a procession of boats and around 10,000 spectators. The lead boat, *Lively*, carried dignitaries and musicians playing *Rule Brittania*. It took 1 hour 40 minutes to reach Marsden.

The canal carried coal, stone, bricks, limestone, corn, pig iron and general merchandise although it never equalled the volume carried by the nearby Rochdale . Shareholders rarely received a good dividend, as the company was never commercially successful. From the late 1830s, the railways began to take an ever increasing share of business. By 1844 the company was forced into a merger, and became the Huddersfield and Manchester Railway and Canal Company.

At Standedge a parallel rail tunnel was dug at a higher level, using the canal for drainage. Cross passages, used to remove spoil to boats, speeded up work, cuting construction time and saving the railway thousands of pounds. After this rail tunnel opened in 1849, a twin was planned but not finished until 1871. A third rail tunnel with double tracks (which is still in use today) was dug on the other side of the canal.

Although closed by Act of Parliament in 1944, the canal tunnel was still navigable. The current restoration programme which began in September 1999 is designed to modern safety specifications. By October 1999 the tunnel had been drained and fenced off. Roadways were under construction at both ends to allow vehicles and heavy machinery access to the tunnel to carry out restoration work.

Two metre rock bolts (as used in mines) were driven into the walls of unlined sections to stabilise the rock. Sediment was pumped out at the Diggle end to settle out in lagoons formed from the canal. Tons of sludge were de-watered and removed to landfill.

The project is scheduled to finish in April 2001.

Standedge tunnel runs from Diggle, northeast of Manchester, to Marsden on the Yorkshire side of the Pennines.

STROOD

Thames & Medway Canal
3,608 m (3,946 yds) – Opened 1824
Converted to rail 1845 – no towpath

At 3,946 yards (3,608 m), Strood in Kent was physically the second longest canal tunnel in the country. It was also one of the shortest-lived; it operated for only twenty-one years before half the tunnel width was converted to a rail track. Narrowboats and trains made uneasy partners, however, and after a few months the canal was filled in and a double rail track installed.

Today, the tunnel is the property of Railtrack and thus access on foot is prohibited for safety reasons. Strood is sometimes known as Higham tunnel, after the old village by its western portal. A local restoration group, the Thames & Medway Canal Society, is active and has restored a length of the old waterway. Unfortunately, it is extremely unlikely that Strood will ever return to its original function.

Strood tunnel lies beside the village of Higham, just west of Rochester in Kent.

SUMMIT

Birmingham Canal Navigations
94 m (103 yds) – Completed by the Dept. of Transport in 1974
Fully navigable – with towpath

In the 1970's, the traffic was routed away from the Galton bridge which crosses Telford's Main Line. The change required the construction of a modern dual carriageway spanning Telford's and Brindley's canals. Instead of building an expensive high-arch or suspension bridge, the decision was taken to fill the valley and build the road on top. To facilitate this,

▲ *The west portal*

each canal was covered with long, prefabricated concrete tubes, which were then earth-filled over the top. These structures are now known as Summit and Galton tunnels.

Galton and Summit afford the highest headrooms of any tunnels in the UK. They boast generous towpaths and sufficient width for boats to pass inside. The Wolverhampton portal of the tunnel is attached to Summit Bridge, hence its name. Despite its position in Britain's second city, the approach to the east portal is surprisingly rural in tone.

Summit, on the Brindley Line canal, and its sister tunnel Galton on the adjacent Telford's Birmingham Main Line are located between Birmingham and West Bromwich, just east of the M5 motorway.

TARDEBIGGE

Worcester & Birmingham Canal
530 m (580 yds) – Completed by John Woodhouse in 1810
Fully navigable – no towpath

Tardebigge is famous in canal folklore for the Tardebigge Locks, and as the place where Tom Rolt moored his boat, met Robert Aickman and founded the Inland Waterways Association. Throughout the centuries, the tunnel has remained in the shadows.

Construction of the tunnel was delayed when the company building the Worcester & Birmingham canal ran out of funds. A new injection of money eventually allowed work to resume.

The north portal

Thomas Cartwright, the canal's chief engineer probably began the tunnel excavations, but it was his successor, John Woodhouse, who completed the project in 1810. Acrimonious negotiations with rival canal companies, particularly the BCN, neutralised the advantage of the canal's broad-gauge tunnels by combining them with narrow-gauge locks.

The south portal

Tardebigge has unlined sandstone sections within the tunnel, and even though a comparative late-comer, no towpath was provided for. Legging was therefore the order of the day until the 1870s, when a steam tug was introduced to pull craft through. This service lasted until the early twentieth century.

Regular commercial traffic ceased in the early 1960s, but Tardebigge tunnel and the Worcester & Birmingham in general have survived to benefit from the growth in tourism.

Tardebigge is situated about two miles east of the Birmingham suburb of Bromsgrove just off the A448

TUEL

Rochdale Canal
98 m (107 yds) – Completed by DCT Engineering Ltd in 1996
Navigable (time restrictions) – no towpath

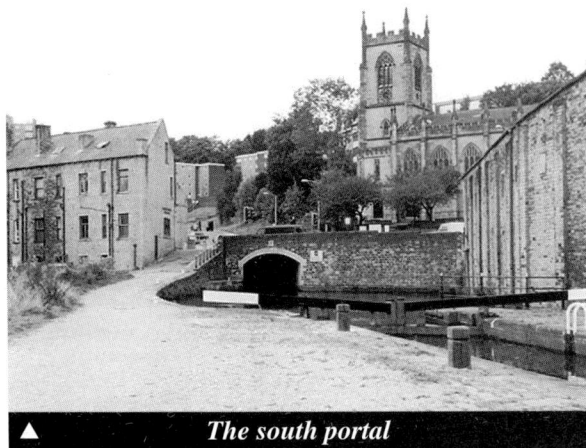

The south portal

Forming the junction of the Rochdale canal and the Calder & Hebble navigation, Sowerby Bridge was historically an important and prosperous canal town. Commercial traffic survived through the area until 1939. This section of the canal was officially closed in 1952. Modern building development during the 1960s obliterated Sowerby Long Tunnel, the original structure of William Jessop.

The revival of the Rochdale's fortunes required the construction of a new tunnel. The line of the canal through Sowerby Bridge was dug out again in 1995 and given a concrete top for the road to run over. Tuel tunnel therefore came into existence on completion of the project a year later.

Navigating the tunnel from the Calder and Hebble canal, approaching via locks 1 and 2 of the Rochdale canal, the entrance is straight and leads into what was Lock No. 3. The curved section bends the canal into line with the bottom gates of the new double-depth lock beside Tuel Lane.

Unlike Jessop's tunnel, Tuel does not boast a footpath, as safety considerations arising from the deepness of the new lock understandably restrict public access.

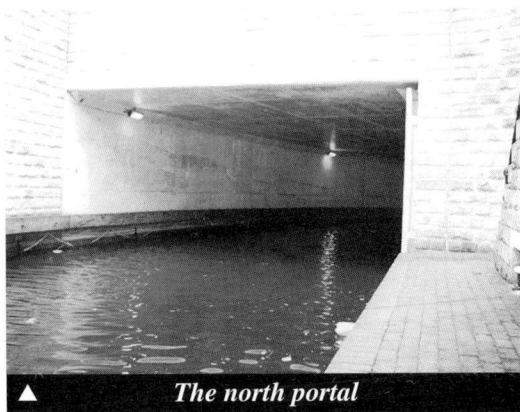

The north portal

Tuel tunnel runs in a curve below Tuel Lane in the centre of Sowerby Bridge in West Yorkshire.

WAST HILL (KING'S NORTON)

Worcester & Birmingham Canal
2,493 m (2,726 yds) – Completed by Thomas Cartwright in 1797
Fully navigable – no towpath

Confusingly, Wast Hill tunnel is also known as "Westhill" and "Kings Norton" (to say nothing of occasional confusion caused by mis-identification with the nearby Brandwood tunnel).

▲ *The north portal*

Part of the Worcester & Birmingham project, work started on the tunnel at Wasthill in October 1795. The line was surveyed by John Snape and Josiah Clowes, but the company engaged Thomas Cartwright as chief engineer for the actual construction. Difficulties caused by the rival BCN company led to broad tunnels and narrow locks; nevertheless, when the stretch was opened to traffic on 27 March 1797 it allowed 60-70 ton barges to navigate as far as Hopwood.

Around 1875 a company tug was introduced to pull all boats through the tunnel, in common with other Worcester & Birmingham tunnels such as Tardebigge and Shortwood.

▲ *The south portal*

Around the turn of the century, the steam tug was replaced by diesel. This in turn was gradually rendered obselete before many decades had passed, as more and more craft became self-powered.

Wast Hill remains tricky to navigate, as vision is obscured within the tunnel. The severe winter of 1978-9 resulted in temporary closure.

The tunnel begins in Kings Norton, just off the A441 and emerges into the countryside beyond.

WELLOW

Somerset Coal Canal
370 m (405 yds) – Completed by William Smith in 1799
Abandoned

Wellow lay on the Radstock Arm of the Somerset Coal canal. The Somerset Coal canal was authorised by an Act of 1794, and opened in its entirety five years later.

The engineer, William Smith, had begun his working life as a surveyor, then acquired experience as an assistant on canals further north. He appears to have been a competant engineer, but Smith's real fame lay ahead of him. Work on the canal tunnels of the Somerset Coal canal (perhaps even Wellow itself) led him to develop an interest in geological strata.

The Somerset village of Wellow lies between Bath and Trowbridge.

WOLFHAMPCOTE

Oxford Canal
30 m (33 yds) – Completed by Samuel Simcock circa 1774
Abandoned 1834 – there was no towpath

Samuel Weston, in a report on the Oxford canal in 1778, was of the opinion that Wolfhampcote need not have been dug at all. It was certainly a small tunnel (33 yards) and a cutting or bridge might well have sufficed.

However, the engineer responsible, Samuel Simcock, had served his apprenticeship under James Brindley and was an experienced man. Brindley himself had surveyed the line of the Oxford canal, including Wolfhampcote, but had almost certainly died before work on this particular tunnel began.

In 1834 Wolfhampcote suffered the same fate as the old Newbold tunnel further north on the canal; both were abandoned when fourteen miles of meandering waterway were cut through by a straighter line.

Any remains that survive lie near to the more famous tunnel of Braunston on the Grand Union.

Wolfhamcote lies on a line between Rugby and Daventry, west-south-west of Braunston.

WHITEHOUSES

Shropshire Union Canal (Llangollen Section)
175 m (191 yds) – Completed by Thomas Telford in 1802
Fully navigable – with towpath

The line of the Llangollen Canal (as it is popularly known) was first surveyed by two local contractors, William Turner and John Duncombe, then by William Jessop. The sponsors of the project attracted so much interest that the company was over-subscribed. Jessop was appointed chief engineer, with Duncombe and Turner as his assistants, together with Thomas Denson. A young Thomas Telford was later added to the staff.

The north portal

Telford's influence and reputation grew, particularly with the bold and successful design of the nearby Chirk aqueduct. When Jessop left the project in 1801, Telford took over as chief engineer. He and Denson were therefore technically responsible for Whitehouses tunnel, which was opened in 1802.

Like so many other waterways, the early success of the canal began to suffer severe competition from the growing railway network. Traffic gradually declined until the canal was officially abandoned in 1944. By 1947, Tom Rolt could not even reach Whitehouses tunnel due to the collapse of a nearby cutting.

Happily, local enthusiasts, supported by Wrexham Rural District Council, saved both canal and tunnel from extinction. Conditions have improved steadily since the re-classification of the Llangollen in 1968.

The south portal

Whitehouses tunnel lies on the border between England and Wales. The A5 road passes over the top.

WHITTLE HILLS

Lancaster Canal
236 m (259 yds) – Completed by John Rennie circa 1804
Abandoned circa 1840 – the modern concrete towpath is fenced off

The Lancaster canal was a peculiar entity; particularly as it was constructed and functioned in two halves never physically joined with one another. After surveys and proposals in the 1770s, it was not until June 1792 that actual work was finally authorised. John Rennie was appointed chief engineer, with Archibald Millar as his resident and the notorious John Pinkerton as contractor.

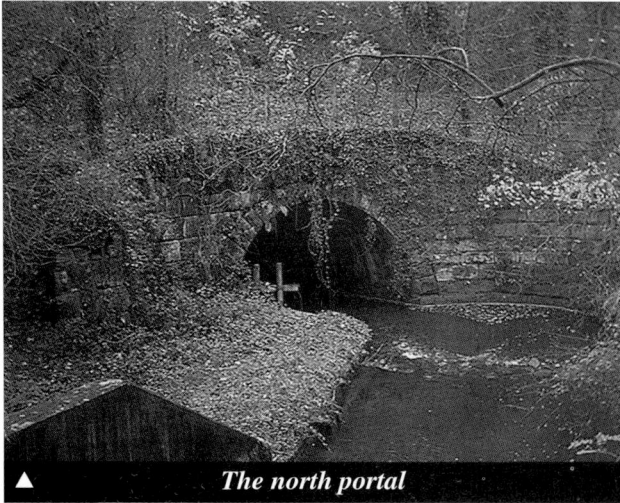
▲ *The north portal*

A reorganisation in 1795 placed Henry Eastburn in office as resident engineer of the southern section, but various problems continued to delay construction. By 1800, William Cartwright had replaced Eastburn, and it was almost certainly he who finally saw the Whittle Hills tunnel completed. There is clear evidence within the tunnel of an original portal, indicating that the tunnel was extended at some time during its short life.

The southern section of the Lancaster was by this time a confusing interconnection of canal, tramroad and railway. A railway track placed beside the canal in 1837 strangled trade so much that the canal company ceased commercial carrying on the southern section in 1840.

The Lancaster canal was purchased by the LNWR railway company in 1885, by which time Whittle Hills was almost certainly abandoned. Today it lies in the middle of fields, in the shadow of the M61 motorway.

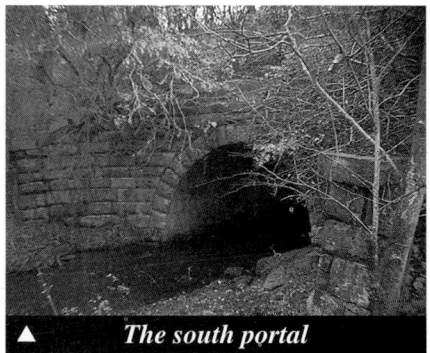
▲ *The south portal*

The tunnel is situated on the western side of the M61, between Chorley and Preston, a short walk from the Johnson's Hillock locks on the Leeds & Liverpool canal.

WOODLEY

Peak Forest Canal
161 m (176 yds) – Completed by Benjamin Outram circa 1799
Fully navigable – with towpath

Work began on the Peak Forest canal following an Act of Parliament in March 1794. Digging began from both ends of the canal simultaneously, and as Woodley lies in the middle it was evidently one of the last features to be completed.

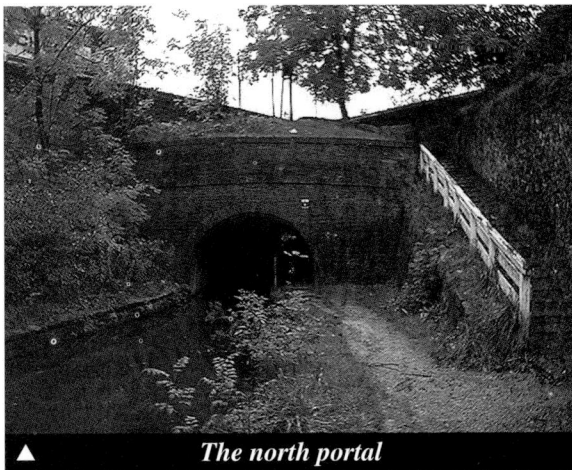

The north portal

In the intervening years, the chief engineer, Benjamin Outram had suffered from the interference of the canal company and frequent meddling from an American engineer, Robert Fulton, who had impressed the directors. However, by the time Woodley was completed, Benjamin Outram had seen off Fulton, and thus the credit for the tunnel goes to the chief engineer and his resident assistant, Thomas Brown.

After these initial problems, the Peak Forest canal enjoyed a lengthy period of prosperity, transporting coal, limestone and textiles from the north-west. Serious competition from the railways began in 1838, when a line was opened between Manchester and London, and income from the canal began to decline.

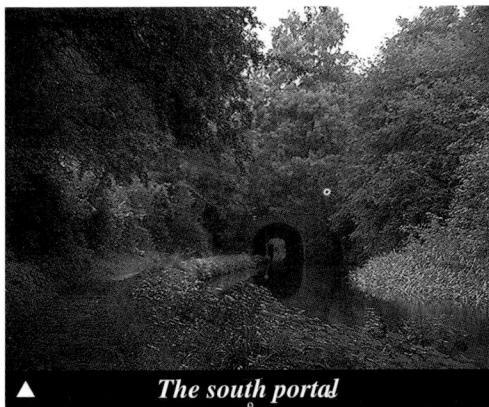

The south portal

Commercial traffic ceased by 1958 and the canal looked doomed; but the efforts of enthusiasts finally impressed the authorities, and the waterway was saved. A fully restored canal re-opened in March 1974, but without the old nameboards proclaiming the name of the tunnel – "Butterhouse Green Tunnel".

Woodley tunnel lies on the Cheshire Ring, just south of Ashton-under-Lyne and Manchester.

WORSLEY MINES

Bridgewater Canal
Approximately 74,000 m (81,000 yds) total
Completed by John Gilbert and James Brindley circa 1761
Closed to the public – no towpath

Worsley Mines are argueably both the oldest and longest total length of any mentioned in these pages. The twin canal tunnels disappear into a sheer rockface and merge after about 500 metres. They then lead to a maze of tunnels and mineworkings.

Although some might argue the tunnels at Worsley Delph to be simply a flooded set of mineworkings, they are central to the history of canal engineering. Coal had been dug at Worsley for hundreds of years before the 3rd Duke of Bridgewater turned it into a serious commercial operation. In 1759 Bridgewater's agent John Gilbert and his brother Thomas introduced the Duke to James Brindley, and a famous partnership was born.

Engaging Brindley as consultant engineer and Gilbert as resident supervisor, Bridgewater financed the building of a canal into the mineworkings at the Delph and outwards to cross the River Irnham. This allowed coal to be brought to the market much more cheaply than before. When Parliament permitted Bridgewater to extend his canal into Manchester the price of coal halved, but the venture still more than repaid the investment.

The warren of underground workings continued to be developed for over a century, resulting in side branches, loading bays & wharves on several levels, joined by locks, shafts and an inclined plane. The width varies widely throughout the network as there are loading wharves and caverns. The 'starvationer' boats operating in the tunnels (such as the sunken craft still seen today beside the left-hand tunnel entrance) were typically 4½ ft wide. The underground workings have remained exactly as they were left in 1889 with occasional inspections. There have been calls to open parts to tourism but, at the beginning of the twenty-first century, such developments still seem far off.

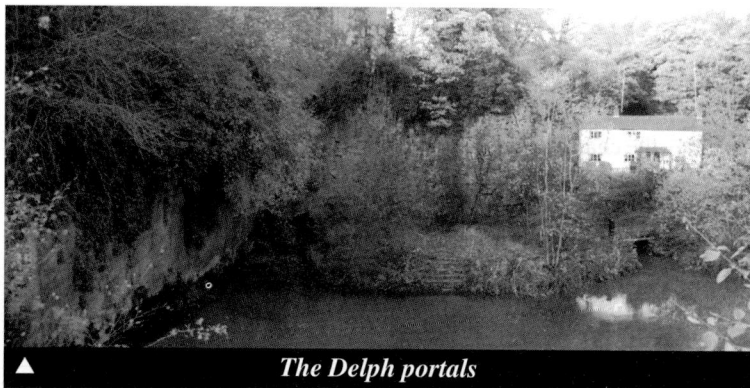

The Delph portals

The entrances to the mines can be seen from Worsley Road (A572). Worsley is situated on the western outskirts of Greater Manchester.

122

YARDLEY

Warwick & Birmingham Canal
256 m (280 yds) – Opened 1796
Opened out – unlikely to have had a towpath

The Grand Union Canal into the centre of Birmingham was originally built as the Warwick & Birmingham canal. Its purpose was to create an alternative to the Worcester & Birmingham route north, as traffic on the latter canal used to jam up when it reached the Worcester Bar at Gas Street Basin. Worcester & Birmingham traffic intending to link to the Birmingham & Fazeley canal also faced a further bottleneck at the top of the Farmers Bridge flight of 13 locks.

Approaching from the outskirts of Birmingham, the old Warwick & Birmingham canal passes through Acocks Green and bends east to the south of Yardley to avoid a large ancient cemetery on high ground. Here a tunnel of 256 m (280 yds) was constructed through the hilllside. It was opened in 1796.

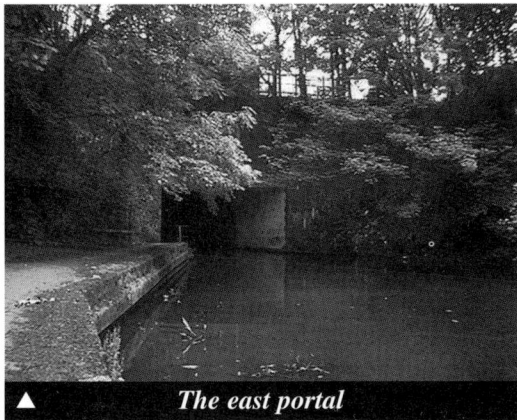

The east portal

The tunnel would have been used extensively to bring tea from what was then Ceylon to the Ty-Phoo wharves at Digbeth. The canal thus provided an unbroken waterway from Birmingham city centre to Columbo over 10,000 miles away.

The tunnel was later opened out and replaced by a deep cutting with a bridge to carry the main road (now the B4146) over the canal. The bridge was rebuilt in 1935 with an uninterrupted towpath. At some time the bridge has been widened on both sides, as can be seen by the changing profile viewed from the canal; first square, then oval, then back to square.

Today the road has a strip of land with trees and shrubbery on either side between the footpath and the tops of the portals, giving it the appearance of a miniature tunnel.

The west portal

Yardley tunnel lies just south of the crossroads of the A45 Birmingham-Coventry road and the A4040 "outer circle" of Birmingham.

Sapperton (Coates portal)

Tunnel Ghosts

From the digging of the first tunnel, the mysterious, gloomy world under the earth quickly brought forth fearful stories of ghosts and spirits. Some, it is said, were the souls of hapless workers, many of whom are known to have died in accidents during the construction of our tunnels. Other shapes are the remains of leggers and lengthmen, suffocated or drowned, and yet more ghostly forms have also been reported, all doomed to relive terrible deeds and ghastly horrors until the end of time...

It is no accident that Tom Rolt, perhaps the most famous observer of British canals, was also well known in other circles as a writer of ghost stories. Ghosts and canal tunnels appear to have a mutual attraction.

Harecastle I – north portal

The term "Kit Crewbucket" has now become accepted slang for a canal ghost, although its precise origin appears to eminate from the northern portals of the tunnels at Harecastle. In Victorian times, the town north of the tunnel, Kidsgrove, was known to canal folk as "Kitcrew", while a "buggut" was a dialect term for a ghost (rather similar to the Scottish "boggle"). According to one story, two local men murdered a woman and threw her corpse into the Trent & Mersey canal. She now appears to frighten the unwary, manifesting either as a headless body, or in the form of a white horse. Tom Rolt himself reported conversations with several old boaters who claimed to have seen the apparition.

The Harecastle ghost may not be the only one of its type on the canal network, for Saddington, a lonely tunnel on the Leicester section of the Grand Union, is said to be home to another headless woman, whose appearance portends doom and disaster.

Saddington – north portal

Slightly less threatening is the ghost who wanders up and down the towpath north of Crick tunnel further along the Leicester section. This is a male ghost, said to be the shadow of a drowned lengthman. Some canal writers such as Hugh McKnight claim that this spectre is friendly, but many of the villagers are not so sure. We can only hope that this particular "Kit Crewbucket" continues to ensure the safety of canal users, as he would have during his life.

126

Inside Berwick

If any tunnel really does possess a ghost, it must be the isolated Berwick tunnel on the derelict Shrewsbury canal. Early in the twentieth century, a murder victim was dropped down one of the ventilation shafts of the abandoned tunnel. The authorities thoughtfully took measures to stop up the shaft, ensuring that there would be no repeat of the incident.

Further south on the Basingstoke canal, the 12,500 bats of Greywell tunnel are said to share their dark abode with a mysterious phantom. Was it responsible for the disastrous collapse in the tunnel in 1932, which virtually ensured that this tunnel will never see another narrowboat?

Welsh waterways have their share of wraiths - none more so than the towpath at Pontcysyllte, near to the tunnels of Whitehouses and Chirk. Sensitive visitors might glimpse a beautiful lady in crinolines, although she disappears if approached.

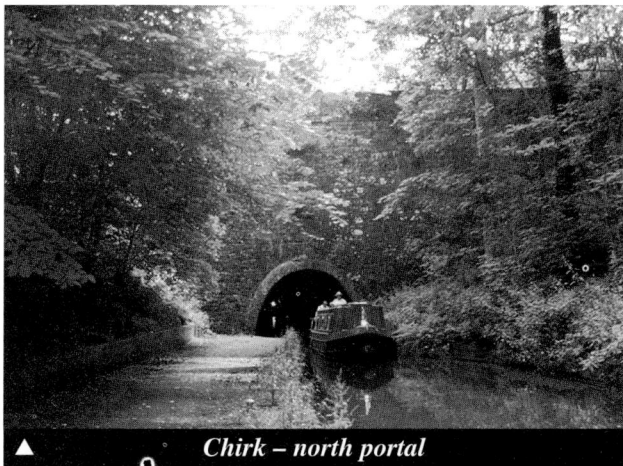

Chirk – north portal

Finally, the most noble "Kit Crewbucket" of all has often been seen riding across his lands near Worsley tunnels. On certain nights, it is said that a coach and spectral horses carry a lordly passenger across the moors. Those brave enough to look at the face peering back at them have reported it to be none other than the Duke of Bridgewater himself.

Of course, no boater should allow any of these tall tales to deter them from entering a tunnel on our waterways. No intelligent person *really* believes in ghosts....

...do they?

Index